BEASTLY ABODES

Design: Dana Irwin
Photography: Richard Babb and Bill E. Duyck
Gallery Photography: Evan Bracken
Production: Elaine Thompson
Drawings: Don Osby
Cover Design: Karen Nelson

**Library of Congress Cataloguing-in-Publication Data
Available**

10 9 8 7 6 5 4 3

A Sterling/Lark Book

First paperback edition published in 1996 by
Sterling Publishing Company, Inc.
387 Park Avenue South, New York, N.Y. 10016

Produced by Altamont Press, Inc.
50 College Street, Asheville, NC 28801

© 1995 by Altamont Press

Distributed in Canada by Sterling Publishing
  c/o Canadian Manda Group, One Atlantic Avenue, Suite 105
  Toronto, Ontario, Canada M6K 3E7
Distributed in Great Britain and Europe by Cassell PLC
  Wellington House, 125 Strand, London WC2R 0BB, England
Distributed in Australia by Capricorn Link (Australia) Pty Ltd.
  P.O. Box 6651, Baulkham Hills, Business Centre, NSW 2153,
  Australia

Every effort has been made to ensure that all the information in this
book is accurate. However, due to differing conditions, tools, and
individual skills, the publisher cannot be responsible for any injuries,
losses, and other damages which may result from the use of the information in this book.

Printed in Hong Kong

Sterling ISBN 0-8069-3168-X Trade
           0-8069-3169-8 Paper

BEASTLY ABODES

Homes for Birds, Bats, Butterflies & Other Backyard Wildlife

BOBBE NEEDHAM

Sterling Publishing Co., Inc.   New York
A STERLING/LARK BOOK

C O N T

I am afoot with my vision…
Where the bat flies in the Seventh-month eve…
Where the bee-hives range on a gray bench in the garden
half hid by the high weeds …
Solitary at midnight in my back yard, my thoughts gone
from me a long while.
—WALT WHITMAN, "SONG OF MYSELF"

INTRODUCTION

I'VE WONDERED AS I'VE BEEN WRITING *Beastly Abodes* THIS WINTER, IN A LITTLE HOUSE PERCHED ON the side of a mountain in Western North Carolina, whether I might be sending out vibes sympathetic to various members of the animal and avian world.

Many mornings I've seen a small shadowy body through the glass of one of the bird feeders, too still to be a bird, and after a while I'll go out and wave the chipmunk off; he scampers down the hemlock trunk, his cheeks bulging with sunflower seeds. Gray squirrels, of course. A huge raccoon that came for a while at night and wrapped himself around one of the feeders to scoop out the seeds. Indoors, in the weeks before Christmas I caught and released from my Hav-a-hart trap in a warm cupboard by the stove thirteen deer mice, quite beautiful brown-and-white creatures with big ears and soft shoe-button eyes.

More birds have visited my feeders and heated birdbath this year than last, even though it's a much warmer winter: besides my faithful chickadees, tufted titmice, and clutch of mourning doves, I've regularly seen a pair of white-breasted nuthatches; nearly every day a red-bellied woodpecker and a pair of downeys have come to hang lopsided on the suet feeder and a flock of goldfinches have crowded the thistle feeder's perches; and pine siskins, Carolina wrens, a song sparrow, a white-throated sparrow, and male and female cardinals have occasionally dropped by. Crows flap through the trees to march up and down the driveway in the cold as if they're waiting for a bus.

So I've felt blessed by the natural world during this period of writing, as well as by the creative spirit of the designers of the homes in the book.

Our first concern in creating these abodes has been functional: to design a home a creature can actually nest and thrive in or in which creatures can rest and recuperate. At the same time, we have aimed for a natural look both to blend with and enhance the backyard environment. With a few exceptions, the basic plan of each abode follows closely recommended guidelines for homes for each creature, based on the research and experience of naturalists. (The exceptions are noted in project descriptions—for instance, the small bat attic by Robin Clark is his own experimental design; the Bat Conservation Association encourages such experiments, as long as they follow basic bat preservation guidelines. Other exceptions are the skeps, which no bee could live in; they are purely decorative.)

To increase your chances of bringing house and creature together, each abode project includes a description of at least one of the species for which it is designed, along with tips for siting the house. If you like the idea of an owl or bat box, for instance, you can see what species might live in your area, whether you can provide the kind of habitat they prefer, and so on. Then you can avoid the almost certain disappointment you would experience if you had built and hung your beautiful screech owl house, for example, on the wall of your Dallas townhouse, or put a bat house five feet up a fir tree in a nice shady spot in your Michigan backyard.

GALLERY

SOME BEASTLY ABODES MORE THAN OTHERS APPEAL TO OUR ARTISTIC SENSE, AND SOME ARE DESIGNED FOR AESTHETIC APPEAL ONLY, LIKE THE ONES IN THIS "GALLERY." These pieces don't appear among the projects—they're here simply to please your eye and maybe stimulate your creative juices. (The toad houses are the exception—they are functional, a dressed-up version of the book's kids' toad houses.)

ELMA JOHNSON

FERN LETNES AND HENRY BAKER/
LADY SLIPPER DESIGN

LADY SLIPPER DESIGN

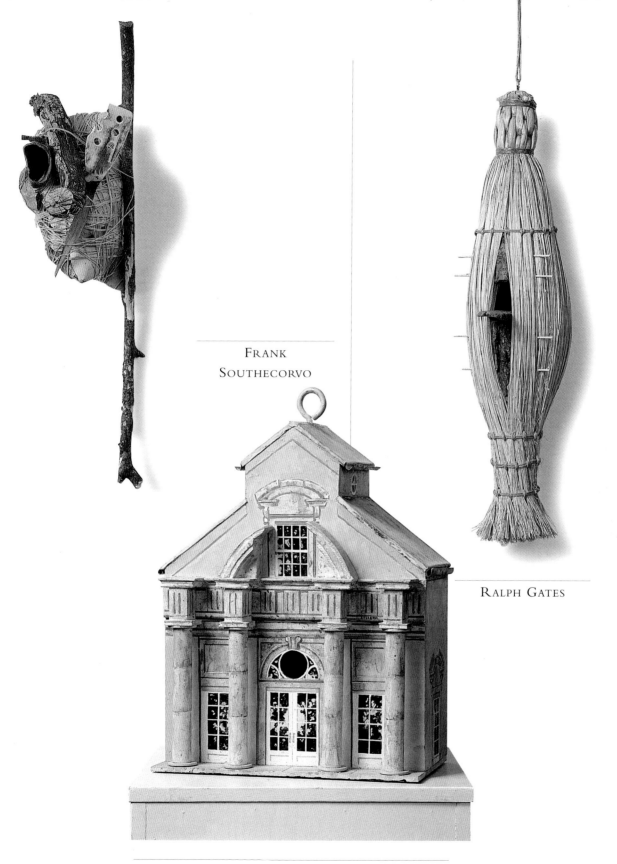

FRANK
SOUTHECORVO

RALPH GATES

CHUCK O'CONNELL

NELS ARNOLD

TYGRE

SUE WHEELER

MIMI SCHLEICHER

MARIE HUDSON

RANDY SEWELL

CAROL BOMER

CAROL SUTHERLAND

DAN FREDERICKS

BEASTLY BASICS

I HOPE THE PROJECTS IN *BEASTLY ABODES* INSPIRE YOU TO ADAPT, DESIGN, decorate, and otherwise take off from the basic patterns. At the same time, I know anyone who's going to take the trouble to build an abode wants to be sure not only that creatures will live in it but that they will thrive. And since a well-made nest box should last ten years or more, here are some general tips and reminders to make any abode stronger, safer, and more functional.

FOR THE BIRDS

▪ The only birds who prefer perches are house sparrows and European starlings, two species dangerous to song-birds. As cute as a perch might look on a nest box, experts strongly advise leaving it off.

▪ To keep rain (and some predators) out of nest boxes, be sure that the front edge of the top overhangs by at least 2" and that the sides enclose the floor (that is, don't nail the sides to the top of the floor).

▪ Birdhouses need good ventilation. Drill at least two five-eighths-inch holes near the top of the front and of both sides.

▪ If you don't want mice to move in to your songbird boxes after the nesting season,

leave a side or the front open through the winter.

▪ Metal roofs, much less entire metal houses, can overheat so badly in direct sun that eggs or young are damaged. (But aluminum martin houses are okay.)

FOR ALL CREATURES

▪ When possible, use cedar, redwood, or cypress for the large nest boxes; pine is okay for small boxes, although cedar is an excellent choice for any box. Wood treated with green preservative poses a threat to wildlife who move in—its copper base combines with water to create poisonous vapors. It's a good idea to occasionally coat the backs of houses with a safe preservative, since they are the part most vulnerable to dampness.

▪ Where you can, hinge part of a nest box (a side or roof, not the bottom) for easier checking and cleaning. Keep the hinged section closed with nails with large heads—raccoons can open boxes fastened with hooks and eyes.

▪ Don't allow any paint or stain to get inside a nest box.

▪ The best way to attach an abode to a living tree is to use lag bolts and washers, so you can unscrew them slightly each spring to allow for tree growth.

▪ Clean out nest boxes in late fall (unless project notes advise you not to). Remove old nests and debris and scrub the inside. Many creatures use these abodes for protection in the winter, so you may want to leave nest boxes or roosts out for them.

HOSTING WILDLIFE

HOW CAN YOU ENTICE WILDLIFE—OR MORE WILDLIFE—ONTO YOUR property? Simply put, the more varied the habitat you can offer, the more wildlife species you can expect to show up.

Specifically, water. Food. Water. Cover. Water. Nesting sites. Water. Get the idea? What host would fail to offer a guest, at the very least, a drink—in winter a warming cup of coffee or tea, in summer a cold beer or a refreshing glass of water or lemonade? If we want wildlife to keep coming back, we need to provide water, cover, and food; if we want wildlife to come and stay, we also need to offer them places to build nests.

The ideal way to invite wildlife to stay, like any other guests, is to cater to their tastes—that is, to turn your property, or part of it, into something like the mix of flowers, herbs, weeds, grasses, trees, shrubs, and vines that occurs in their natural habitat.

So we're not talking about just any old flowers, herbs, weeds, grasses, and so on. Library shelves are bulging with books telling you what to plant, when, where, how much, and for whom. State departments of wildlife and agricultural extension agents are other excellent free sources of information.

In a nutshell: Copy nature. A few rules of thumb, some more obvious than others:

- The native wildlife of your area will thrive best on the native plants of your area. Happily, native plants often ask less of you than fancy imports in terms of maintenance.

- The more habitat edges you can create, the more wildlife you are likely to have. An edge is where one kind of habitat meets another—where grass meets trees, or where a flower garden meets shrubbery. And the more like natural edges these are, the better, which means curving lines and irregular borders.

- Ape nature by combining different heights of plants—tall and short trees, tall and short shrubs, flowers, ground cover.

WATER

The good old birdbath still works fine as a water source for many of the creatures you'd probably like to have as visitors to your garden or yard. In my urban Florida backyard a few years ago, every night for most of a summer a mother raccoon led her three kits over my roof, down the pecan tree, and onto the screened porch for cat food; to top off the evening they climbed into the birdbath and knocked it off its pedastal. Besides birds and raccoons, birdbaths serve squirrels, opossums, and chipmunks. A tip: Songbirds are suckers for the sound of dripping water.

It's as critical to make water available in winter as in summer, especially in freezing temperatures. While most small mammals hide out for short cold spells, birds must eat and drink every day to live, and many species must bathe frequently to free their feathers of dirt and oils no matter what the thermostat reads.

Butterflies can't drink directly from open water. For them you can supply areas of damp sand or earth.

If you have the space and the energy to create a small pool, it will draw an even greater variety of wildlife—frogs and turtles, bats, rabbits, perhaps some waterbirds.

FOOD

As many of us who have bird feeders will be more than delighted to tell you, one can enjoy an entertaining variety of wildlife with nothing on offer but food. All kinds of birds, as well as chipmunks, ground squirrels, flying squirrels, and raccoons, visit feeders year round.

A variety of natural food sources will only increase the

variety of your wildlife guests. Plants that provide fruit, nuts, or seeds at different times of year are sure bets, along with berry-bearing shrubs and vines. Many butterfly larvae thrive on thistle, milkweed, and other wild plants (see the section on butterflies). Cutting down on or, even better, cutting out insecticides harmful to birds and animals is equally important.

SHELTER AND NEST SITES

One of the premises of this book is that wildlife need more safe places to take shelter from predators or bad weather and to bear and raise their young. You can make your yard safer and more attractive to lizards and chipmunks by adding rock piles or stone walls. Leave the trunks of dead trees standing, and you can look forward to being woken by woodpeckers. Many migrating bird species as well as rabbits use brush piles, tall grass, and dense shrubs for cover or nest sites. Squirrels and some birds take shelter and build nests in evergreens, while other birds, such as robins, nest in low trees and shrubs. Bats and butterflies often nest and roost behind loose bark. Besides natural shelter and homes, of course, handmade homes like those in this book offer safe haven and nesting sites for a marvelous variety of wildlife.

If you're not sure what kinds of birds, bats, or other creatures might be enticed to live on your property, the chart "Who Needs What?" should help you decide which abodes it would make sense for you to build.

Carroll Henderson, Minnesota's nongame wildlife supervisor, was responsible for the first of the booklets now offered by many state departments of natural resources (variously called wildlife commissions, fish and game departments, and so on) with plans for the backyard wildlife common to their states; these provide helpful regional information.

HOW TO HOST WILDLIFE
EVEN WITH NO BACKYARD

ONE OF THE JOYS OF HOSTING WILDLIFE IN THE CITY IS KNOWING YOU'RE MEETING A REAL NEED. IF YOU HAVE A BALCONY, A PIECE OF ROOF GARDEN, OR SIMPLY A *window and a window-box planter, you can provide food and water for wildlife—add an outside wall you can attach an abode to and you're a landlord.*

The best vine for cities may be Boston ivy, and birds love its blue fruits. Nandina with its beautiful red fruits and fall foliage can grow almost anywhere, including tubs. Birds flock to the reddish-orange fruits of pyracantha; you can espalier it on a wall or grow it as a shrub. Small hollies work well (be sure you have at least one male plant).

With windows and window boxes, offer hulled sunflower seed in a feeder, one attached either to the window with suction cups or to the wall. In warm weather, plant the window box with bright flowers to entice butterflies and hummingbirds—zinnias, cosmos, marigolds, and lantana for butterflies; scarlet salvia or red petunias for hummingbirds (or red impatiens in a shady box). You can also attach a hummingbird feeder to your window. Put a heavy shallow container in the middle of your window box for water.

If you can attach a nesting shelf to a wall, you may play host to robins, Eastern phoebes, or barn swallows. A nest box may bring a family of house sparrows, starlings, house wrens, titmice, chickadees, or even squirrels. (Check the projects and species notes for height off the ground and nest box specifics.)

WHO NEEDS WHAT?

WILDLIFE	NATURAL FOOD	PREFERRED HABITAT
BIG BROWN BAT	Insects (prefer beetles)	Buildings and trees near meadows, pastures, residential areas
LITTLE BROWN BAT	Aquatic insects (esp. mosquitoes)	Caves, buildings, rock cavities near rivers, marshes, lakes
MEXICAN FREE-TAILED BAT	Insects (mostly moths)	Caves, buildings in/near cities, residential areas, farmlands
BUTTERFLIES	Flower nectar, tree sap, rotting fruit, dung, urine, mud	Varied: gardens, grasslands, farms, streamsides, deciduous woods, orchards, fields, roadsides, etc.
AMERICAN KESTREL	Insects, small mammals, reptiles, amphibians, birds	Open areas, forest edges to cities
AMERICAN ROBIN	Fruits, earthworms, insects	Swamps and open woods, residential areas
BARN SWALLOW	Insects	Farmland, residential areas
BARRED OWL	Small mammals, birds, reptiles	Conifer & deciduous forest, wooded swamps, river valleys
BEWICK'S WREN	Insects, seeds	Gardens, farms, woods, thickets
BLACK-CAPPED CHICKADEE	Insects, seeds, fruits	Wood edges, mixed & deciduous woods, towns, gardens
BLUE-WINGED TEAL	Seeds of aquatic plants, grasses, grain in autumn, aquatic snails, insects	Fresh ponds, marshes
BOREAL OWL	Small mammals, birds	Conifer & deciduous forest, bogs
CANADA GOOSE	Grasses, marsh plants, aquatic plants, grains	Ponds, rivers, bays, fields, saltwater marshes
CAROLINA CHICKADEE	Insects, seeds, fruits	Residential areas, swamps, woods
CAROLINA WREN	Insects, seeds	Gardens, thickets
DOWNY WOODPECKER	Insects	Mixed woods, suburbs, towns
EASTERN BLUEBIRD	Insects, fruits	Farms, wood edges, orchards
EASTERN PHOEBE	Flying insects	Open woods, farms, towns, roadsides
EASTERN SCREECH OWL	Insects, small mammals, birds, fish	Open woods, deciduous forest, parks, towns, scrub; near water
GREAT CRESTED FLYCATCHER	Insects, berries, small lizards, small fruit	Woodlands, groves
HAIRY WOODPECKER	Adult & larval beetles, ants, fruits, nuts, corn	Open woods with mature trees and snags, wooded swamps, residential areas
HOUSE WREN	Insects, seeds	Gardens, farms, woods, thickets
MALLARD	Seeds, leaves	Usually edges of lakes, ponds, reservoirs; sometimes fields

WILDLIFE	NATURAL FOOD	PREFERRED HABITAT
MOUNTAIN BLUEBIRD	Insects, fruits	Open lands
MOUNTAIN CHICKADEE	Insects, seeds, berries	Conifers
MOURNING DOVE	Seeds, grains	Open woods, farmland, residential areas
NORTHERN FLICKER	Ants, other insects, wild fruits	Woods, suburbs
NORTHERN SAW-WHET OWL	Small mammals, insects	Forests, thickets, groves
PLAIN TITMOUSE	Insects, acorns, berries	Shade trees, woods
PURPLE MARTIN	Mostly flying insects	Farms, residential areas, and parks near water
RED-BREASTED NUTHATCH	Insects, seeds	Conifer forests
RED-HEADED WOODPECKER	Insects, acorns, wild fruits	Groves, farms, towns
TREE SWALLOW	Flying insects, berries, seeds	Near water; open wooded swamps
TUFTED TITMOUSE	Insects, seeds, mast,* fruits	Shade trees, deciduous woods, swamps
VIOLET-GREEN SWALLOW	Mostly flying insects	Open forests, mountains, ranches, towns
WESTERN BLUEBIRD	Insects, fruits, berries, weeds, seeds	Deserts, farms, open woods
WESTERN SCREECH OWL	Small mammals, insects, birds, fish, reptiles	Woods, scrub, orchards, woodlots
WHITE-BREASTED NUTHATCH	Insects, seeds, fruits, mast*	Mixed forests to suburbs
WOOD DUCK	Acorns, insects	Wooded swamps, marshes, near water
AMERICAN TOAD	Insects	Loose soil, cool daytime shelter
DEER MOUSE	Seeds, nuts, fruits, green plants, insects	Woodland edges, beaches, brushpiles
FOX SQUIRREL	Pine cone seeds, mast* (?)	Deciduous woodlands
GRAY SQUIRREL	Mast,* seeds, berries, insects, birds' eggs, sometimes nestlings	Deciduous woodlands, esp. oak-hickory-beech; river bottoms, city parks, suburban yards
MASON BEE	Flower nectar, rotting fruit	Gardens, orchards, fields
NORTHERN FLYING SQUIRREL	Mainly underground fungi, lichen; some seeds, buds, flowers; occasional birds' egg	Conifers, mixed woodlands
RED SQUIRREL	Mast,* seeds, berries, flowers, fungi, birds' eggs, sometimes nestlings	Conifer woodlands, esp. spruce-pine-hemlock
SOUTHERN FLYING SQUIRREL	Mast,* fruits, berries, tree buds, insects; occasional birds' egg	Deciduous trees, esp. hickory, maple, beech, oak
WESTERN PAINTED TURTLE	Crayfish, insects, mollusks	Deep pools with muddy bottoms, sunning spots
WHITE-FOOTED MOUSE	Seeds, nuts, fruits, green plants, insects	Woodland edges, logs, brush piles

*Mast includes acorns, beechnuts, and other nuts that accumulate on the ground under trees.

ABODES FOR BATS

"BAT CONSERVATION HAS COME HOME TO ROOST," SAYS NATURALIST ROGER SWAIN IN *SAVING GRACES*. "IF WE ARE EVEN HALF-SERIOUS ABOUT HAVING WILDLIFE CLOSE AT HAND, WE SHOULD BE MAKING ROOM FOR BATS."

WHY BAT HOUSES?

It's a seller's market in the U.S. bat real estate world. Bats don't build their own nesting places or roosts, they simply find a warm, dark place to hang, and the old warm, dark places—caves, abandoned buildings, dead trees, barns, cliffs—are fast disappearing. In many states, various bat species are now endangered.

Apart from the reward of providing homes for the homeless, many of us welcome bat neighbors as natural insect zappers. Depending on what is in season, they gorge themselves nightly on mosquitoes, moths (which produce cutworms and corn earworms), cucumber beetles, June bugs, stinkbugs, and leafhoppers. One little brown bat, for instance, consumes about 500 insects per hour. The fewer bats in the world, the more dependent we are bound to become on toxic insecticides.

DOS AND DON'TS FOR BAT HOUSE SUCCESS

You don't need a big bat house to attract bats. Bat houses only two feet tall and five or six inches deep have drawn nursery colonies (mothers with young) of more than two hundred. What matters most is where you put your bat house.

A recent study by Bat Conservation International (BCI) came up with encouraging news: in the northern third of the United States (where they are most popular), more than four out of five bat houses placed with an eye to bat needs actually had bats in them. This study and various bat house builders' experiences have given us some valuable pointers for bat house success.

■ The three biggest selling points for bat real estate, as for human housing, are location, location, and location—particularly location with reference to the sun. Bats are quite sensitive to variations in temperature.

Northern bats, such as the little brown and big brown, often crave warmth—their houses need at least four hours of sun a day and should be painted a dark color or covered with tar paper. In the South, the Mexican free-tailed bat needs shade and cooler temperatures in summer, especially in lowland desert areas, while hibernating big brown bats need six or seven hours of sun in winter.

the concentration of insects. Anyplace with lots of insects probably also has bats.

▪ Still another point about location: the higher a bat house, the greater the chance that bats will occupy it. Put your house on a fifteen- to twenty-foot pole and see what happens. (If climbing predators—raccoons, cats, or snakes—are a problem, wrap the pole with an eighteen-inch piece of sheet metal three feet above the ground.)

▪ You can also hang your bat house on a tree or on the side of a building, at least twelve to fifteen feet up and with correct sun exposure.

▪ The most successful bat house builders in the BCI study put up houses in groups of three or more. But don't rush to put up a whole bat city until you've observed a few houses for several seasons to see what works.

▪ Bats don't like drafts. If the parts of your box don't fit together snugly, seal spaces with silicone caulk.

▪ Keep each chamber three-quarters to one and one-half inches; be sure the inside chamber walls are rough.

▪ To help bats cling even better, line the vertical partitions of your bat house with fiberglass insect (or window) screening, or with one-quarter-inch hardware cloth. Tilting your house about ten degrees may also help keep baby bats from falling out.

▪ Bat housing is still very much in the beginning stages. All kinds of designs that meet basic temperature and safety requirements may work. Go ahead and experiment! Remember that insulation at the top of a house helps stabilize temperatures, that taller roosting chambers also help reduce the impact of radical changes in outside temperature, and that open-bottom designs last longer than closed-bottom ones and discourage use by squirrels, mice, or birds.

▪ For excellent information on bats, write Bat Conservation International, P.O. Box 162603, Austin, TX 78716.

▪ Particularly temperature sensitive are nursery colonies—groups of mothers with young—which prefer roosts that remain at eighty to ninety degrees Fahrenheit for most of the day and night. Bachelor bats like temperatures ten to twenty degrees cooler, as do females after the young are weaned.

▪ Houses placed within a quarter mile of a stream, river, or large lake are most likely to attract bats because of

SMALL BAT NURSERY

MARK STROM

Anything goes in bat house decor, but the Gothic look of this abode has a certain traditional Transylvanian feel to it.

TOOLS

Circular or table saw
Dado blade (optional)
Jigsaw
3/8" drill
Drill bits (1/16", 3/8")
Staple gun
Protractor
Block plane
Tape measure
Paintbrush
Hammer
Knife

MATERIALS

Exterior T-111 plywood, 3/8" thick:
  Back: 20 x 24-1/4"
  Front & overlay: 20 x 20-1/2" (2)
  Inside partitions: 19-7/16 x 20" (2)
  Top: 7 x 22"
Pine, 3/4" thick:
  Sides: 3-1/2 x 24" (2)
  Ceiling: 3-1/2 x 18-1/2"
  Insulation holders: 7/8 x 18-1/2" (2)

SUPPLIES

1" finish nails
3/8" staples
5/8" brads (18 gauge)
19 x 78" fiberglass screen
Black exterior paint
Exterior stain for overlay
Fiberglass batt insulation scraps
Mirror hangers (2)

BUILDING THE NURSERY

- **STEP ONE** Cut all pieces.
- **STEP TWO** On the two side pieces and the ceiling piece, measure 7/8" from each edge and cut two grooves the length of each piece, 7/16" wide and 1/2" deep. Use a dado blade if you have one, or make several

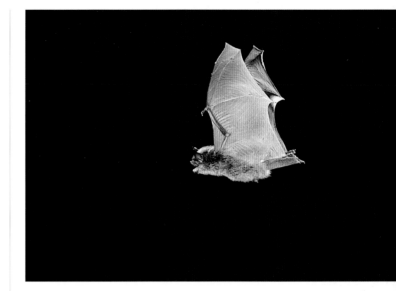

LITTLE BROWN BATS

■

The most common bat house resident in the northern states and most of Canada, little brown bats are about three and a half inches long with a wingspread of about eight inches, ranging in color from brown or reddish brown to gray. You can sometimes spot these small bats hunting insects in the late afternoon as well as at night—they are voracious mosquito eaters.

■

Little browns often roost during the summer in buildings near rivers, lakes, or marshes, where they can fill up on aquatic insects. They mate in the fall, then hibernate, typically producing one young in June or July, which is weaned and flying in three or four weeks. These bats are somewhat more heat tolerant than others and can rear young in temperatures as high as 104 degrees—they choose roosting sites with high, stable temperatures.

■

In late summer, as little browns prepare to hibernate, some colonies travel as far as 200 miles to their chosen cave or mine, where they will stay for the next six to eight months.

■

Along with providing a bat house, you might try wrapping a piece of corrugated sheet metal, about twenty-four by thirty-six inches, around a tree that gets appropriate amounts of sun. This arrangement has attracted nursery colonies of these bats, who may roost between the metal and the tree.

passes through with a table saw, or rout out the grooves with a router and 1/4" straight bit.

■ **STEP THREE** Measure with a protractor and cut a 38° angle on one end of each side piece. (*Note: Be sure that when the sides are placed facing each other, the grooved sides are to the inside, also facing each other, and the cut angles slope in the same direction.*)

■ **STEP FOUR** Use 1" finish nails to attach the back to the rear of the side pieces so its upper edge extends about 1/4" above the points at the top of the angle. Use a block plane to trim that edge to the same angle as the sides.

■ **STEP FIVE** Cut the fiberglass screen into two 19 x 39" pieces. Wrap one piece around each partition panel and tack into place with staples. Use 1" finish nails to attach the ceiling between the sides at the top of the box, even with the edge of the forward angle and with the grooves facing down.

■ **STEP SIX** Measure down 8-1/2" from the bottom of the ceiling and attach one insulation holder against the back and between the sides using 1" finish nails. Lay insulation scraps into the space between the holder and the ceiling. Then slide a partition into each of the grooves, tight against the ceiling. Fasten the second insulation holder in the same manner at the same location, against the forward partition.

■ **STEP SEVEN** Stuff insulation scraps into the space above the ceiling, and place a layer of insulation in the space between the forward holder and the ceiling.

■ **STEP EIGHT** Nail the front piece to the front of the side pieces so its upper edge meets the forward part of the side angles. Trim that edge with the plane if necessary. Using 1" finish nails, fasten the top flush with the back of the box and with a 1" overhang at each side.

■ **STEP NINE** Paint the outside of the box with several coats of black exterior paint.

■ **STEP TEN** On the remaining overlay panel, draw your own design or use the pattern provided. Cut out the openings with a jigsaw. Coat the overlay with exterior stain. Tack the completed piece to the front of the box with 1" finish nails at the edges and 5/8" brads in the center area.

■ **STEP ELEVEN** Fasten two mirror hangers to the rear of the box for hanging. (See "Dos and Don'ts for Bat House Success" on page 18 for tips on mounting and location.)

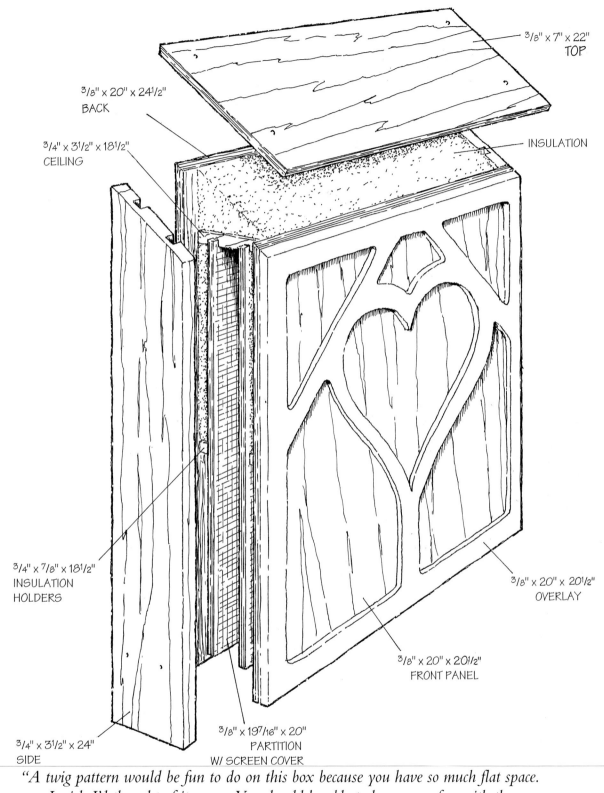

3/8" x 7" x 22"
TOP

3/8" x 20" x 24 1/2"
BACK

3/4" x 3 1/2" x 18 1/2"
CEILING

INSULATION

3/4" x 7/8" x 18 1/2"
INSULATION
HOLDERS

3/8" x 20" x 20 1/2"
OVERLAY

3/8" x 20" x 20 1/2"
FRONT PANEL

3/8" x 19 7/16" x 20"
PARTITION
W/ SCREEN COVER

3/4" x 3 1/2" x 24"
SIDE

"A twig pattern would be fun to do on this box because you have so much flat space.
I wish I'd thought of it sooner. You should be able to have some fun with the
decorating—it's a challenge to make a good-looking bat box."

MARK STROM, WOOD SCULPTOR

LARGE BAT HOUSE

STEVE MITCHELL

This bat house, with its southwestern feel and warm color (for not-too-cold weather), is the size of those especially popular with bats in a Bat Conservation International study.

TOOLS

Handsaw
3/8" drill
1/4" drill bit
Screw bit/countersink (no. 6)
Phillips screwdriver
Tape measure

MATERIALS

Western red cedar, 11/16" thick:
  Front, sides (2), & partitions (5): 11-1/8 x 24" (8 total)
  Back: 11-1/8 x 32"
  Roof: 11-1/8 x 14"

SUPPLIES

1-1/2" decking screws (no. 6)
Exterior wood glue or caulking compound
Dark-colored exterior paint

BUILDING THE HOUSE

■ **STEP ONE** Cut all pieces. Leave the wood surfaces rough.

■ **STEP TWO** Center the two side pieces on the face of the back piece so each is flush with the edges and the back extends 4" above and below the sides. Mark the position of each side piece.

■ **STEP THREE** For hanging, drill two 1/4" holes in the back piece, centered and 1" from the upper and lower edges. Then use a number 6 screw bit to drill four holes spaced 7" apart through the back face and into the edges of each side piece. Fasten the sides with decking screws.

■ **STEP FOUR** Position and mark the five partitions between the side pieces so the upper and lower edges are even and there's a 1" space between partitions. Drill and fasten the partitions in the same manner as the sides.

■ **STEP FIVE** Position the front and align the sides with the edges. Drill and fasten it to the sides as before. The partitions should be secured from the front as well,

MEXICAN FREE-TAILED BATS

■

Mexican free-tailed bats are the most common residents of bat houses in the southern and southwestern United States, ranging as far north as Nebraska, Colorado, Utah, Nevada, and Oregon in the summer and migrating to Mexico and Central America in the winter. Mexican free-tails have large ears, sharp teeth, a wingspan of up to twelve inches, and tails that extend beyond the membrane that connects legs and tail.

■

They are high-speed flyers and so far are known to use only houses mounted on buildings or poles, perhaps to avoid the obstacles around many tree-mounted houses. In hot climates, they have used bat houses mounted on the shaded sides of both stone and wooden buildings. Because they have traditionally reared their young in caves, they may prefer bat houses with spacious interiors covered with hardware cloth or fiberglass screening. Females bear one young a season, most commonly in late May or early June.

■

Mexican free-tails eat enormous numbers of insects, mostly moths.

but only two screws per piece are needed; place them 1" from the ends.

■ **STEP SIX** Apply glue or caulk to the upper edges of the box and the rear edge of the top. Position the top against the back piece and drill two holes 9" apart along each edge using a number 6 screw bit. Fasten with decking screws.

■ **STEP SEVEN** Sand the outside of the bat box. To help it retain more heat in cool weather, paint it a darker color.

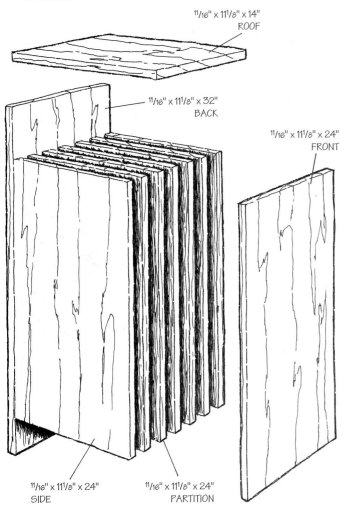

¹¹/₁₆" x 11¹/₈" x 14"
ROOF

¹¹/₁₆" x 11¹/₈" x 32"
BACK

¹¹/₁₆" x 11¹/₈" x 24"
FRONT

¹¹/₁₆" x 11¹/₈" x 24"
SIDE

¹¹/₁₆" x 11¹/₈" x 24"
PARTITION

DEBUNKING SOME BAT MYTHS

■ *Bats aren't blind, although most navigate by echolocation. That is, they emit squeaks, clicks, and buzzes, creating sound waves that bounce off objects in their path.*

■ *Bats rarely carry rabies; because any wild mammal that can be caught, including a bat, may be sick, err on the side of caution and don't handle bats.*

■ *Bats aren't attracted to your hair, although the common brown bat can detect a human hair three feet away.*

■ *Bat droppings will not harm your health any more than do bird or cat droppings. Just don't inhale any of them.*

■ *Putting up bat houses in your yard won't attract bats to your attic. If your attic would make good bat housing, they're already there.*

"I have a kind of kinship with bats, being a spelunker. The most common around here are the eastern pipistrelle—we see them hanging in the caves. Bat houses are important, even for bats like pipistrelles that don't breed in them, because they serve as day shelters. The bats are out feeding sometimes for one or two days, and they'll need places to take shelter until they're ready to return to their colony."

STEVE MITCHELL, WOODWORKER

Bat Attic

Robin Clark

The smallest bat box in the book, this elegant, light-colored attic works best in warmer climates—if hung in a northern climate, it needs to be painted a dark color or covered with tar paper, to absorb and hold heat.

Tools

Circular saw or handsaw
3/8" drill
Screw bit/countersink (no. 6)
1/4" drill bit
Phillips screwdriver
Tape measure
Palm sander
Awl
Paintbrush

Materials

Western red cedar, 11/16" thick:
  Back: 6-3/4 x 24"
  Front: 5-1/4 x 18"
  Sides: 3-3/8 x 21" (2)
  Roof: 4-3/4 x 9-1/4"
  Attic floor: 1-3/4 x 5-1/4"
  Partition: 5-1/4 x 13"

Supplies

1-1/2" decking screws (no. 6)
Exterior glue or caulking compound
Black acrylic paint

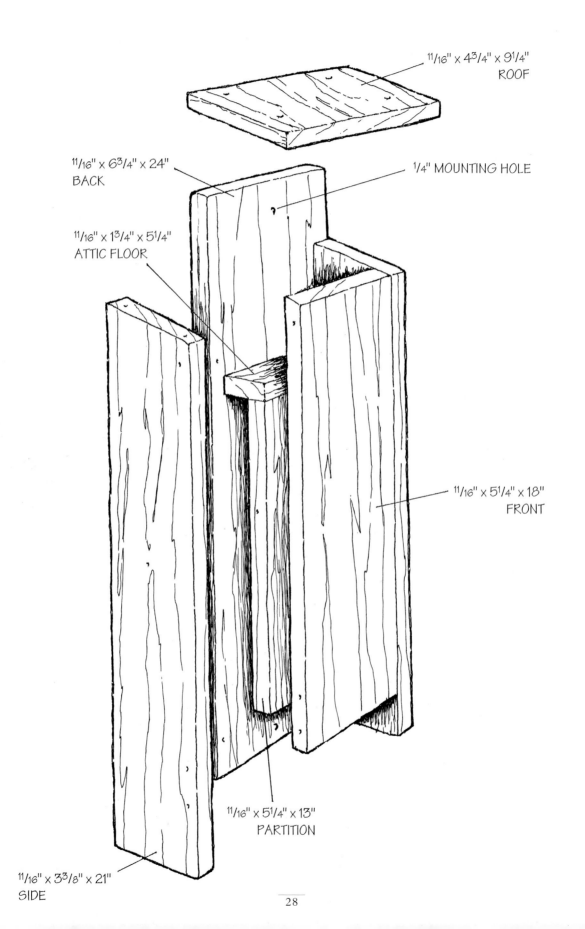

$^{11}/_{16}$" x 4$^3/_4$" x 9$^1/_4$"
ROOF

$^{11}/_{16}$" x 6$^3/_4$" x 24"
BACK

$^{1}/_4$" MOUNTING HOLE

$^{11}/_{16}$" x 1$^3/_4$" x 5$^1/_4$"
ATTIC FLOOR

$^{11}/_{16}$" x 5$^1/_4$" x 18"
FRONT

$^{11}/_{16}$" x 5$^1/_4$" x 13"
PARTITION

$^{11}/_{16}$" x 3$^3/_8$" x 21"
SIDE

BUILDING THE BOX

- **STEP ONE** Cut all the pieces using the diagram and materials list as a guide. One 9-1/4" edge of the roof should be cut at a slight bevel.
- **STEP TWO** Use a number 6 screw bit to drill four pilot holes along the edges of the back, 6" from top and bottom. Use the same bit to drill holes in each side—two 3" and 4-1/2" from the bottom along the front edge, and one 11" from the bottom edge, 1-3/8" from the rear edge. Drill 1/4" holes in the back for mounting.
- **STEP THREE** Use an awl or large nail to roughen the inside surfaces of the side and front pieces and both sides of the partition. Then align the lower edge of the sides and back and fasten from the back with decking screws.
- **STEP FOUR** Lay the box on its back and support the partition on 1"-thick scrap wood. Drill and fasten it from the sides so its lower edge is 3" from the lower edge of the sides. Remove the scrap.
- **STEP FIVE** Position the attic floor at the top edge of the partition, flat against the sides and back. Drill, then fasten from the top and back with four decking screws.
- **STEP SIX** Position the front between the side walls so the upper edges of the front corners are even. Fasten the front with decking screws.
- **STEP SEVEN** Caulk or glue the upper edge of the box and position the roof bevel edge against the back of the box. Drill and fasten from the top with four decking screws.
- **STEP EIGHT** Paint a bat on your box, leave it plain, or decorate it with natural or found materials. (For location and mounting information, see "Do's and Don'ts for Bat House Success," p. 18.)

WATCHING YOUR BATS

OF THE FORTY OR SO BAT SPECIES IN THE UNITED STATES, YOU ARE MOST LIKELY TO FIND ONE OF THREE IN YOUR BAT HOUSE: BIG BROWN BATS AND LITTLE BROWN BATS IN THE NORTH, AND BIG BROWN BATS AND Mexican free-tailed bats in the South.

To see if bats have moved in, check your houses several times a month in summer, once in fall and winter. After they've taken up occupancy, you can check them very briefly with a flashlight without disturbing them—if you are quiet and don't touch the house. You can also use reflected light from a mirror, but keep in mind that such light is terribly bright—just a flash is enough.

To find out how many bats you've got, count them as they emerge from the house at dusk. To see if you have a nursery colony, check the house about forty-five minutes after sundown in late May or early June, and through early July in cold climates—you're looking for little pink shapes with elbows.

"*With the bat attic, I tried to emulate bats' natural habitat, like a dead tree, but with more space to accommodate more bats. I put a divider inside to give them more vertical clinging space. Bats are very sensitive to temperature, so the attic idea—the space above the inside divider— allows them to move from a warmer to a cooler part of the box.*"
ROBIN CLARK, WOODWORKER

Twig Mosaic Bat House

BOBBY HANSSON

Part of the joy of this project lies in searching for the twigs and branches for the mosaic—watch for downed trees, follow tree workers around. Then you get to create your own patterns…experiment with colors and designs…learn the effects of different woods.

TOOLS

Handsaw
Coping or keyhole saw
3/8" drill
Drill bits (1/16", 1/4")
Screw bit/countersink (no. 6)
Phillips screwdriver
Finishing hammer
Tape measure
Knife
Pruning shears

MATERIALS

Twigs or branches of any wood
Oak or pine, 3/4" thick:
    Front: 7-1/2 x 12"
    Back: 7-1/2 x 14"
    Partition: 7-1/2 x 9"
    Sides: 9 x 12" (2)
    Floor: 7-1/2 x 6-1/2"
    Roof: 12 x 12"

SUPPLIES

1-1/2" decking screws (no. 6)
1-1/2" finish nails
3/4" brads (18 gauge)

BUILDING THE HOUSE

■ **STEP ONE** Cut out all the pieces. To give the bats a surface to cling to, score one face of the back with a handsaw to create a series of parallel notches about 1/2" apart.

■ **STEP TWO** Position one side on the edges of the front and back piece with all the top edges flush. The scored back ridges should be facing toward the inside of the box. Use a number 6 screw bit to drill three holes along each edge about 5" apart. Fasten with decking screws.

■ **STEP THREE** Place the partition midway between the front and back and flush to the top edge. Position the remaining side, drill, and fasten as before. Drill two holes through each side to hold the partition and fasten with decking screws.

■ **STEP FOUR** Place the floor piece flush with the box's lower edge and against the front to create a 3/4" entrance space at the rear. Use a 1/16" drill bit to predrill two holes through each side, and drive 1-1/2" finish nails to hold the floor in place.

■ **STEP FIVE** Fasten the major defining branch forks to the front and sides by predrilling 1/16" holes through the branches and fastening with 3/4" brads. Use longer brads if needed, but don't let them protrude through to the inside of the box. Position or trim the upper ends of the branches to allow the roof to be attached later; trim the lower ends to overhang the box edges slightly.

■ **STEP SIX** Fill in the remaining spaces with smaller twigs, creating patterns and color or texture changes as desired. Don't fasten nails too closely to the twig ends, and lay the completed sides on towel padding while working on the opposite faces. Since pine wood is softer than oak, it's a better choice for the front and sides because it accepts nails more easily.

■ **STEP SEVEN** Position the roof even with the rear edge, flush to the back. Predrill four holes. After the box is mounted you can secure the roof with four decking screws.

■ **STEP EIGHT** Drill 1/4" mounting holes near the top and bottom of the back piece. Fasten the roof in place after mounting. (See "Dos and Don'ts for Bat House Success," p. 18, for tips on mounting and siting your house.)

"The creative process takes a long time for me. I'll think about building a bat house, and then maybe I'll be at someone's house or see a picture and that will set it off. With twig mosaic, part of it is finding those special pieces of wood that make it beautiful."

BOBBY HANSSON, WOOD ARTIST

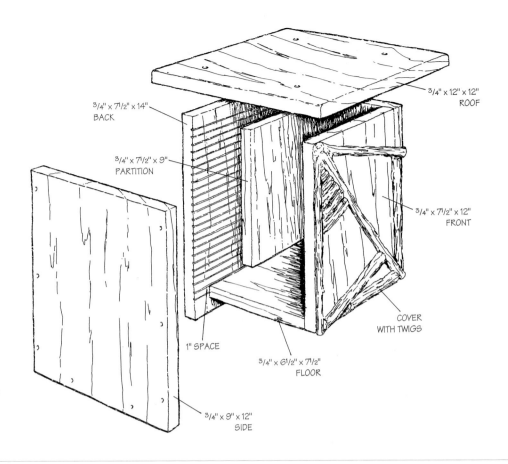

3/4" x 7 1/2" x 14"
BACK

3/4" x 12" x 12"
ROOF

3/4" x 7 1/2" x 9"
PARTITION

3/4" x 7 1/2" x 12"
FRONT

COVER
WITH TWIGS

1" SPACE

3/4" x 6 1/2" x 7 1/2"
FLOOR

3/4" x 9" x 12"
SIDE

BIG BROWN BATS

At four and one-half inches and with a wingspread of about twelve inches, the big brown bat species is somewhat larger than the little brown bat. Its range includes Canada and most of the United States, except the extreme southern portions of Florida and Texas. After the little brown bat, these are the most likely bat house residents, sometimes overwintering in houses as far north as New York.

■

Colonies of big brown bats often roost behind chimneys, under eaves, or in building walls, as well as behind loose tree bark and in tree hollows. These bats feed on a variety of insects, swooping over meadows and pastures and among the trees and streetlights of towns and cities.

■

Mating in fall and winter, big brown bats produce one or two young a year, in late May or early June, forming nursery colonies of 20-300. They are known to abandon roosts when temperatures rise above 95° Fahrenheit. The young fly within a month.

RUSTIC BAT HOUSE

ROLF HOLMQUIST

"Some of the wood I use is 150 years old. It's all from old barns—the older it is, the more character it has. And the older I get, the more I appreciate old things—I hate to see things just disappearing."

ROLF HOLMQUIST, ARTIST

TOOLS

Handsaw
3/8" drill
Drill bits (1/8", 1/4")
Screw bit/countersink (no. 8)
Hammer
Clamps
Tin snips
Phillips screwdriver
Tape measure

MATERIALS

Note: The widths of the front and back pieces can vary, as long as their width below the roof totals about 20-1/2" for the front and about 21-1/2" for the back.

Found wood and bark of any species for finishing
   touches
Barn wood (or other found wood) of any thickness
   (here, 1"):
   Top: 6 x 18"
   Sides: 2 x 21-1/2" (2)
   Top frame: 2 x 11-1/2"
   Bottom: 1-1/2 x 11-1/2"
   Front: 8–12-1/2 x 15-1/2" (2)
   Back: 10–11-1/2 x 15-1/2"
   Ledge: 1 x 11-1/2"

SUPPLIES

2-1/4" decking screws (no. 8)
1/2" staples
15 x 23" fiberglass window screening
6 x 6" galvanized sheet metal
1/2" wood screws (no. 4)
Found items (here, decorative brass, metal hanger straps, pennant)
Exterior wood glue

BUILDING THE HOUSE

- ■ **STEP ONE** Cut all pieces.
- ■ **STEP TWO** Place the sides against the top frame and bottom piece. The lower edge of the bottom should be 1/2" or so from the end of each side, and flush with one surface of the frame. Drill through at the corners and fasten with glue and decking screws.
- ■ **STEP THREE** Drill 1/4" mounting holes through the center of the back pieces that you will place at the top and bottom of the frame. Then position the back pieces on the frame, centered and flush with the ends of each side. There should be a 3/4" entrance gap between the bottom and the back. Drill two holes per board with a number 8 screw bit and fasten with decking screws.
- ■ **STEP FOUR** Trim and staple the screening to the back, top frame, and sides of the partially assembled box.
- ■ **STEP FIVE** Center the front pieces on the frame, flush with the upper ends of each side. When placing the final piece, leave a 3/16" gap between it and the board above. The lower edge of this final board should be flush with the bottom piece.
- ■ **STEP SIX** Center the roof on top of the box with its rear edge flush with the back. Drill six holes with a number 8 screw bit and fasten the roof using glue and decking screws.
- ■ **STEP SEVEN** Add your own ornaments and natural objects to the roof and face of the box. Use glue and small screws to attach pieces of bark or other objects to the face and sides. (See "Dos and Don'ts for Bat House Success" on page 18 for mounting and siting tips.)

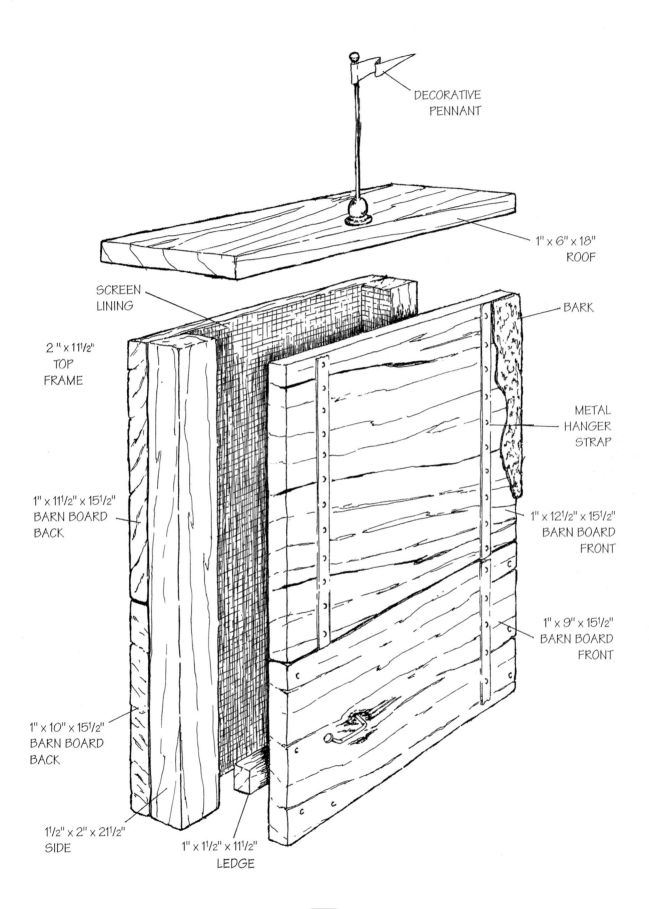

DECORATIVE
PENNANT

1" x 6" x 18"
ROOF

SCREEN
LINING

BARK

2 " x 11½"
TOP
FRAME

METAL
HANGER
STRAP

1" x 11½" x 15½"
BARN BOARD
BACK

1" x 12½" x 15½"
BARN BOARD
FRONT

1" x 9" x 15½"
BARN BOARD
FRONT

1" x 10" x 15½"
BARN BOARD
BACK

1½" x 2" x 21½"
SIDE

1" x 1½" x 11½"
LEDGE

ABODES FOR BUTTERFLIES

To survive winter, butterflies must either migrate south or hibernate. For protection from the cold, the species that overwinter choose dark sheltered places—inside barns, behind bark in trees or woodpiles and, sometimes, in butterfly hibernation boxes like the ones in *Beastly Abodes*. They often hibernate from late August to April or May. During the spring and summer months, butterflies may use these boxes for protection from birds and other predators.

What to Do

Once you've built your butterfly box, place pine bark mulch or tree bark *loosely* inside it, standing up. In warm weather, mount the box at a height of three to four feet, near flowering plants—ideally, mount it on a pole or post. In winter, when ten species of butterflies in the mainland United States hibernate, place the box in a sheltered spot protected from wind.

Who to Expect

Among the more common species of U.S. butterflies that hibernate as adults—and thus that may choose to overwinter in your butterfly box—are mourning cloaks, comma anglewings, queens, question marks, red admirals, painted ladies, American painted ladies, and western painted ladies (also called West Coast ladies).

Mourning cloaks prefer to eat tree sap and often lay their eggs on the twigs of poplars, willows, or elms. To feed, they typically land on the trunk above the sap and crawl down to it. They also sip flower nectar, fruit, and mud. Resident in most of the Northern Hemisphere, they average three inches, with rich brown wings bordered by blue dots, with an outer lacy border of light yellow. You may spot them sunning, wings spread, in early spring.

Hibernators among the thistle butterflies, who frequent thistles and whose spiny larvae often feed on them, include **red admirals**, **painted ladies**, **American painted ladies**, and **western painted ladies**.

Common throughout the Northern Hemisphere, red admirals are both migrators and hibernators as adults. Their intricate wing patterns include bright orange streaks across their upper wings and bordering the bottom half of their lower wings. Adults flock not only to the purple spikes of butterfly bushes but to sap, fruit, dung, and other flowers; red admiral larvae feed on stinging nettles.

The American painted lady, whose wings look like a Tiffany window of mostly dark golds, oranges, brown, and black, has two large eyespots on the underside of each hindwing. Painted and western painted ladies have five spots each. The western painted lady is common

west of the Rockies, the others throughout North America. All are about the same size, two inches, and all lay their eggs on everlasting and burdock; larvae are black with yellow stripes. Painted lady larvae build web nests on their food plant (usually thistle), while western painted lady larvae feed on mallows.

The **queen** butterfly, a smaller, darker brown version of the familiar monarch (about three inches), occurs in the United States mainly in open woodlands, fields, and deserts of the Southeast and Southwest. Queens overwinter only in the South. Female queens hold the butterfly record for matings in one season: up to fifteen times. The larvae, brownish with brown and yellow stripes, feed on milkweed.

The wings of the **question mark** and **comma anglewing**, like those of other members of the Anglewing family, look to me as if someone took small ragged bites out of their edges. Underneath, their wings resemble bark or dead leaves, good camouflage in the woods where they hang out. Both occur east of the Rockies, have spiny larvae, and are darker colored in the summer. Question marks, about two and one-half inches, are named for the silvery mark on the underside of their hindwings. Their larvae feed mostly on elms, while the larvae of the smaller comma anglewings (about one and three-quarters to two inches) eat nettle and hops.

TWIG MOSAIC BUTTERFLY BOX

BOBBY HANSSON

This twig mosaic box delights the eye with a natural symmetry that befits the butterflies it will host.

TOOLS

Handsaw
Jigsaw or keyhole saw
3/8" drill
Screw bit/countersink (no. 6)
1/16" drill bit
1/2" spade bit
Phillips screwdriver
Finishing hammer
Tape measure
Knife
Pruning shears

MATERIALS

Twigs and branches of any species
Pine, 3/4" thick:
    Front: 6-1/2 x 21"
    Back: 6-1/2 x 24"
    Floor: 6-1/2 x 6-1/4"
    Sides: 8 x 24" (2)
    Roof: 10 x 11"
    Roof block: 6-3/8 x 6-3/4"
    Inner strip: 2 x 20"

SUPPLIES

1-1/2" decking screws (no. 6)
1-1/4" finish nails
3/4" brads (18 gauge)
Clear wood finish (optional)

BUILDING THE BOX

■ **STEP ONE** Cut all pieces.

■ **STEP TWO** Mark the locations on the front for the seven entrance slots, three in a triangular pattern at the top and four in a diamond pattern at the bottom. Drill 1/2" holes at the ends of each slot and cut out the openings with a jigsaw.

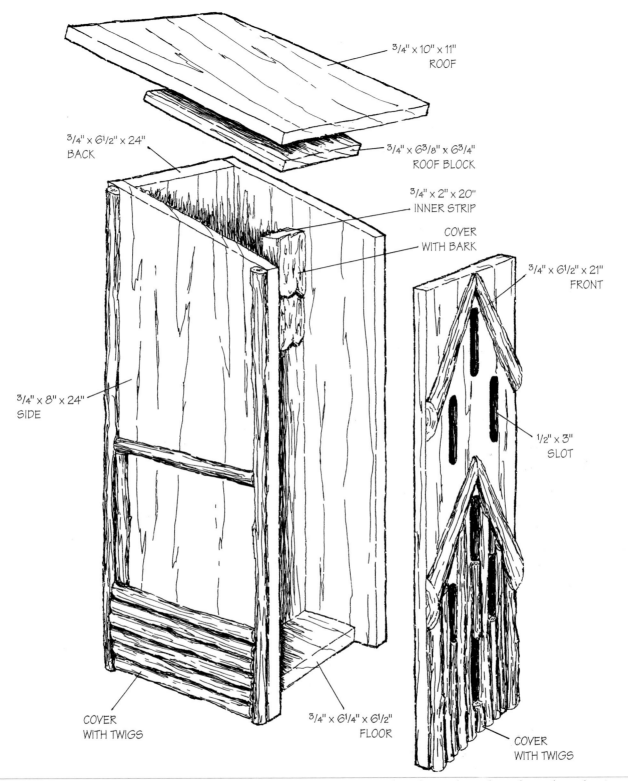

3/4" x 10" x 11"
ROOF

3/4" x 6 1/2" x 24"
BACK

3/4" x 6 3/8" x 6 3/4"
ROOF BLOCK

3/4" x 2" x 20"
INNER STRIP

COVER
WITH BARK

3/4" x 6 1/2" x 21"
FRONT

3/4" x 8" x 24"
SIDE

1/2" x 3"
SLOT

COVER
WITH TWIGS

3/4" x 6 1/4" x 6 1/2"
FLOOR

COVER
WITH TWIGS

"I don't cut branches for my projects. I follow the tree surgeons around and snatch up branches when they're sweeping up. Sometimes you get very exotic trees. A friend called me once to tell me they were making firewood out of an Italian boxwood that had gone down in a storm—they use that wood for making wood engravings."

BOBBY HANSSON, WOOD ARTIST

- **STEP THREE** Fasten the inner strip to one side piece using 1-1/4" finish nails. To give the butterflies something to cling to, attach chunks of bark to the strip with 3/4" brads.
- **STEP FOUR** Position the side pieces flush to the front of the box and drill fastening holes along the edges about 5" apart. Fasten with decking screws.
- **STEP FIVE** Slip the floor into position with a small gap toward the front, and place the back piece between the sides. Drill holes along the back edges about 5" apart, and drill holes through the sides into each edge of the floor piece. Fasten all pieces with decking screws.
- **STEP SIX** Select some slightly curved branch sections about 1/2" to 3/4" in diameter to define the peaks of the two groups of entrance openings. Use the remaining lengths to make uprights and trim for the box corners. Predrill all branches with a 1/16" drill bit, and fasten the branch pieces with either 3/4" brads or 1-1/4" finish nails.
- **STEP SEVEN** Fill in the remaining spaces with smaller branches and twigs in a pattern that you find pleasing. Fasten each piece down before going on to the next.
- **STEP EIGHT** Center the roof block on the roof, drill two pilot holes from the inside, and fasten the block with decking screws. Place the roof on top of the box. A clear wood finish applied to the outside will brighten the bark. (For mounting location and tips, see "What to Do," p. 36.)

HATCHING BUTTERFLIES

I DON'T KNOW OF ANYTHING MORE MAGICAL AND INSPIRING THAN THE METAMORPHOSIS OF A CATERPILLAR INTO A BUTTERFLY. TO WATCH THIS DRAMA FROM opening curtain to finale, you need a caterpillar, or larvae; the leaves it eats; some moisture; a can; and patience. Later you'll need to make a simple cage.

Common butterfly species lay their eggs on particular plants (usually trees), and it is often on the undersides of their leaves that you'll find caterpillars. Some of these plants/trees and the butterfly larvae they host are milkweed, dogbane (monarch); cow parsnip, fennel, dill (swallowtails); cottonwood, wild cherry, willow, maple, alder (tiger swallowtail); willow, cottonwood (mourning cloak); birch, alder, willow, gooseberry, currant, wild rhododendron (anglewing); cabbage, mustard, nasturtium (cabbage white); thistle, pearly everlasting (painted lady).

When you have found a caterpillar, put it in a large can along with some of the kind of leaves it was feeding on. Clean and add fresh leaves as needed, along with some twigs. A caterpillar sheds its skin several times as it grows—when it sheds all its legs except those on its first three segments, it has reached full growth and will soon begin to spin its cocoon, attaching it to a twig or the bottom of the can.

The pupa (cocoon or chrysalis) stage lasts from ten days to eight months, depending on the species (this is where the patience comes in). You can move the pupae to a cage at this point—a cylinder of wire screen or one-quarter-inch hardware

cloth upended on a paper plate with another paper plate for a top. Put a layer of peat moss or soil at the bottom, and spray the chrysalis from time to time with water to keep it from drying out (don't soak it).

Watch for movement and change in the appearance of the cocoon, because the hatching process can be quite short. Don't interfere. Although it may pull itself from the cocoon in only a few minutes, the emerging butterfly needs time to pump air and blood through its body and wings, and its outer skeleton needs to harden. The butterfly is usually ready to fly in about half an hour.

WHAT ATTRACTS WHOM?

SOME PLANTINGS FOR A BUTTERFLY GARDEN

ALFALFA	*Eastern black swallowtail, orange sulphur, dogface, large wood nymph*
ASTER	*Checkered white, common & orange sulphur, question mark, painted ladies, red admiral, buckeye*
BLACK-EYED SUSAN	*Great spangled fritillary, pearly crescentspot*
BUTTERFLY BUSH	*Swallowtails, mourning cloak, comma anglewing, painted ladies, red admiral*
DAISY	*Pearly crescentspot, red admiral, queen*
DANDELION	*Cabbage white, common sulphur, comma anglewing, red admiral*
DOGBANE	*Spicebush swallowtail, checkered white, common & orange sulphur, gray hairstreak, spring azure, pearly crescentspot, mourning cloak, American painted lady, buckeye*
GOLDENROD	*Common & orange sulphur, gray hairstreak, American painted lady, red admiral, viceroy*
LANTANA	*Swallowtails, cabbage white, Gulf fritillary*
LUPINE	*Common blue*
MARIGOLD	*Milbert's tortoiseshell, American painted lady*
MILKWEED	*Swallowtails, checkered & cabbage white, common & orange sulphur, gray hairstreak, spring azure, pearly crescentspot, common blue, great spangled fritillary, question mark, mourning cloak, painted ladies, red admiral, viceroy, monarch, queen*
MINT	*Swallowtails, cabbage white, gray hairstreak, painted ladies, red admiral, monarch, large wood nymph*
PRIVET	*Spring azure, painted ladies, red-spotted purple*
PURPLE CONEFLOWER	*Silvery blue, great spangled fritillary*
QUEEN ANNE'S LACE	*Eastern black swallowtail, gray hairstreak*
RED CLOVER	*Cabbage white, great spangled fritillary, painted ladies, red admiral*
SCABIOSA	*Painted ladies*
SWEET PEA	*Gray hairstreak*
SWEET PEPPERBUSH	*Spicebush swallowtail, question mark, American painted lady, red admiral*
THISTLE	*Swallowtails, dogface, Gulf fritillary, pearly crescentspot, Milbert's tortoiseshell, American painted lady, red admiral, viceroy, monarch*
VERBENA	*Great spangled fritillary*
WINTER CRESS	*Checkered white, gray hairstreak, spring azure, pearly crescentspot*

CEDAR BUTTERFLY BOX

ROBIN CLARK

A handsome box with especially clean lines, this project has a hinged front panel so you can easily check on your guests.

TOOLS

Circular saw
Jigsaw
3/8" drill
Screw bit/countersink (no. 6)
1/4" drill bit
Tape measure
Protractor
Wire-cutting pliers

MATERIALS

Redwood or red cedar, 11/16" thick:
  Roof: 6-3/8 x 7"
  Sides: 5-1/4 x 23" (2)
  Front: 3-3/4 x 22"
  Back: 5-1/4 x 23-1/2"
  Bottom: 4 x 4-3/4"
  Divider: 3-1/2 x 14-3/4"

SUPPLIES

1-1/2" decking screws (no. 6)
4" of copper wire (12 gauge)

BUILDING THE BOX

■ **STEP ONE** Use the illustrations as a guide to cut the front, sides, bottom, and divider. With a protractor, measure and mark a 17° angle on the top edge of the back and the rear edge of the roof. Cut bevels in these pieces.

■ **STEP TWO** Measure and mark out the 1/2 x 3-1/4" slots as indicated in the front door. Use a 1/4" drill bit to bore the ends of each slot, then cut out the slots with a jigsaw.

■ **STEP THREE** Line up the sides with the top and edges of the back piece and use the number 6 screw bit to drill six pilot holes from the back side. Fasten with decking screws. Drill 1/4" mounting holes through the back, 1/2" and 18" from the lower edge.

■ **STEP FOUR** Fit the bottom in place 1" from the back's lower edge. Drill and fasten from the back and

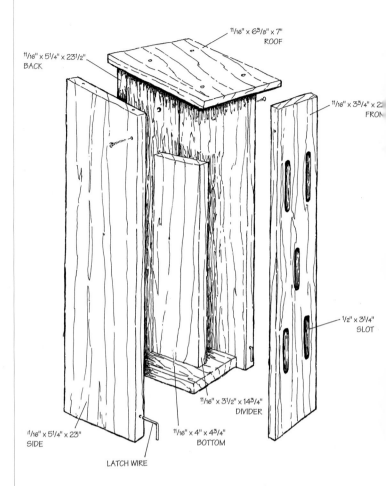

sides. Position the divider in the center of the back piece so its lower end meets the bottom. Drill and fasten from the back side with decking screws.

■ **STEP FIVE** Place the roof so its rear edge is flush with the back, then drill four pilot holes through it and into the side pieces. Fasten with decking screws.

■ **STEP SIX** Drill number 6 pilot holes into the box's front edges 1-1/2" from the lower edge of each side. Cut two 2" lengths of copper wire and bend each at 90°. Push one end of each wire into the pilot holes.

■ **STEP SEVEN** Position the front door so it's flush with the front edges and 1/16" clear of the roof. Drill pilot holes through the sides 1-3/8" from the underside of the roof and loosely fasten the door with two decking screws so it can pivot upward freely. The bent wires at the bottom latch it closed. (For mounting and siting tips, see "What to Do," p. 36.)

*"The key to getting any backyard habitat occupied is to get the house up—
the more you have up, the more chance some will be occupied."*

ROBIN CLARK, WOODWORKER

BARK BUTTERFLY BOX

NONA DONOHO

Since butterflies often choose to roost or over-winter behind loose bark, they should flock to the familiar look of a box like this one.

TOOLS

Jig saw
3/8" drill
Screw bit/countersink (no. 6)
Drill bits (1/16", 1/4")
Hammer
Phillips screwdriver
Tape measure

MATERIALS

Pine bark and branches
Spruce, 3/4" thick:
  Roof: 9-1/4 x 12-1/2"
  Roof block: 5-1/2 x 5-3/4"
  Floor: 5-1/2 x 5-3/4"
  Front: 5-1/2 x 28"
  Back & sides (2): 7-1/4 x 30" (3 total)
  Inner strip: 2 x 24"

SUPPLIES

1-1/2" decking screws (no. 6)
1-1/2" brads (16 gauge)
7/8" brads (18 gauge)
Exterior wood glue
Brown acrylic exterior paint
Clear acrylic sealer

BUILDING THE BOX

■ **STEP ONE** Follow the diagram to cut out all eight pieces of the house.

■ **STEP TWO** Mark the locations as indicated on the front piece for the seven 1/2 x 3" entrance slots. Drill 1/4" holes at the ends of each slot and cut out the slots with a jigsaw.

■ **STEP THREE** Drill the fastening holes in the sides

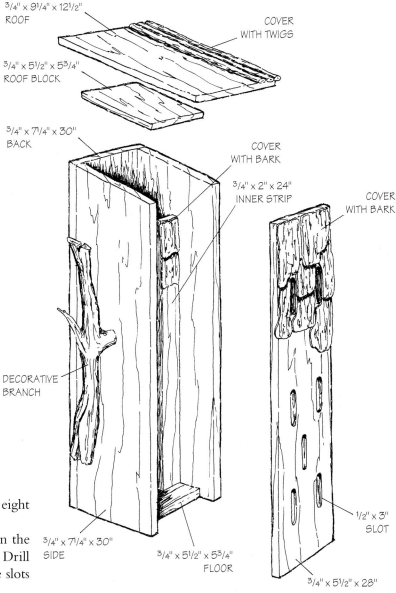

3/4" x 9¼" x 12½"
ROOF

COVER WITH TWIGS

3/4" x 5½" x 5¾"
ROOF BLOCK

3/4" x 7¼" x 30"
BACK

COVER WITH BARK

3/4" x 2" x 24"
INNER STRIP

COVER WITH BARK

DECORATIVE BRANCH

1/2" x 3" SLOT

3/4" x 7¼" x 30"
SIDE

3/4" x 5½" x 5¾"
FLOOR

3/4" x 5½" x 28"

"For this box, I thought bark would give a nice natural texture and be right for the butterflies. But you could paint flowers all over it instead, that should attract them too."

NONA DONOHO, DESIGNER

CREATING
A BUTTERFLY GARDEN

ENTRANCED BY THE BEAUTY AND FRAGILITY OF BUTTER-FLIES, I THINK WE SOMETIMES FORGET THAT, LIKE ALL CREATURES, THEY HAVE A PRACTICAL USE—THEY pollinate plants (they're also an important link in the food chain, but perhaps we can be forgiven for not dwelling on that).

Probably the best way to start creating a space that will attract butterflies is to spend some spring and summer days exploring the neighborhood or countryside or urban area around your home in search of butterflies. And of course you can ask around, as well. What species of butterfly hang out locally?

On what plants? In how much sun or shade?

Butterflies don't need anything fancy or expensive. Just a large, open, sun-filled area; some flowers, for adults; some food sources, for caterpillars (if you want to provide for the butterfly's whole life cycle); shelter; puddles; and rocks. You might consider planting a herb garden if you enjoy herbs—many butterfly species do too. Reserving a section of your yard for native flowering plants and for weeds like dandelion, nettle, and milkweed should also help guarantee a good variety of butterflies. It's best to avoid using any pesticides at all.

One note for dedicated gardeners who may be appalled at the idea of actually inviting caterpillars in for lunch: very few butterfly species cause harm to garden plants. If they do become a nuisance—for instance, if cabbage whites are decimating your nasturtiums—picking the larvae off by hand is a simple task.

About puddles. Butterflies can't drink from birdbaths or other open water. But give them a damp spot of wet sand or dirt and they'll often flock around it. In some species, young bachelor butterflies most commonly exhibit this "puddling" behavior—perhaps the equivalent of visiting the local pub after work.

Butterflies need shelter from predators and wind. Ideal are hedges; groups of small trees or shrubs; or walls, fences, or trellises covered with vines. Possible plantings include honeysuckle and butterfly bushes; and for vines, passion flower, pipevine, or hops. (For what to plant for various butterfly species, see "What Attracts Whom?" page 41.)

and back pieces using a screw bit. Attach the inner strip to one side of the box using 1-1/2" brads, then glue and tack 6" pieces of pine bark to the inside face of this strip using 7/8" brads.

■ **STEP FOUR** Assemble the box so the front is flush to the side edges. Use decking screws to join the back and floor to the sides, leaving a small gap in the floor at the forward part of the box.

■ **STEP FIVE** Center the roof block on the roof section and fasten it using two decking screws. Cut 3/8" branches in lengths of 10-12" and use a 1/16" bit to drill holes through each one. Fasten them to the roof with glue and 7/8" brads.

■ **STEP SIX** Place the roof in position and lightly paint the sides, the back, and all sawn edges with the brown acrylic.

■ **STEP SEVEN** Locate a couple of split-limb branches about 24" long. Use the number 6 screw bit to drill a hole in each one at an appropriate mounting point and drill corresponding holes through each side of the box. Mount the branches to the sides with decking screws held from the inside with a stub or offset Phillips screwdriver.

■ **STEP EIGHT** Collect fallen pine bark or bark from fallen trees and use glue and 7/8" brads to fasten it to the front of the box.

■ **STEP NINE** Spray the entire box with several coats of clear acrylic sealer. (For tips on mounting and siting, see "What to Do," page 36.)

ABODES FOR BIRDS

OFFER BIRDS SOMETHING GOOD TO EAT, SOME LIQUID RE-
FRESHMENT, AND A COMFORTABLE PLACE TO SETTLE, AND
YOU'LL HAVE MORE COMPANY THAN YOU CAN HANDLE.

ABOUT FOOD

The best approach to feeding backyard birds is to provide different kinds of feeders and a variety of food year
round. A good basic plan includes a water source, a
hanging sunflower seed feeder, a tray feeder (or the
ground, if cats aren't a threat) for cracked corn and
mixed seed, and a suet feeder (in cold weather only).

Your feeders may pull many birds through the coldest
days of the year, when juncos, chickadees, finches, titmice, and other winter residents need lots of food
before sundown to survive the night.

ABOUT FLORA

Some simple ways to attract a variety of birds:

- Make a brush pile or two in a place you're willing to
leave them.

- Leave an unmowed section of tall grass, perhaps
twelve feet square.

- Don't cut down dead trees or dead limbs, if they're
not dangerous.

- Plant a patch of wildflowers.

- Leave a piece of your property wild—weeds, underbrush, and all—or let a piece go back to nature.

The conditions that attract wildlife in general, detailed in
the opening pages of *Beastly Abodes*, apply to birds. The
greater the variety of habitats you can provide, the more
birds you can expect to become temporary or permanent
guests. In your long-range plan, aim for providing nest
sites at many heights as well as plants that produce berries
or seeds birds will eat. Ground level plantings might
include some red flowers for hummingbirds, alpine straw-
berry, clover, vetch, grass. Good shrubs include honeysuckle, barberry, juniper, currant, bush cherry, cotoneaster.
For small trees, consider hawthorn, juniper, crabapple,

dogwood, camphor, locust, redbud. Among tall trees, possibilities include pine, spruce, or hemlock for shelter and cones; birch, ash, elm, and maple for seeds; cherry and mulberry for berries; and oak for nuts.

BIRD CRISES

LOST BABY BIRDS

Once you have nests in your yard, you're likely one summer day to find a fledgling (that is, a baby bird with feathers) crouched under a bush or hopping around under a tree, apparently abandoned. The most helpful thing you can do is leave it alone and keep predators away. Even if you can't spot them, the parents are usually hovering nearby and will take care of it. If you must move it to a safer place, though, don't worry that handling it will make the parents abandon it—that's a myth. If the bird has clearly fallen from its nest, you can gently put it back. If the whole nest has fallen down, try to replace it.

BIRDS IN DISTRESS

Hard-hearted as it may seem, the best thing you can do for a sick or hurt bird is let it recover (or not) on its own. If you can't bear not to help it, call the local humane society, ASPCA, Audubon group, or wildlife official for advice. No matter how pure our motives, federal law makes it illegal to keep any kind of wild bird in captivity without a special license.

If your cat or dog captures a bird and you rescue it alive, put it in a safe place—if it's a fledgling, return it to its nest, if you can. My only experience in this area was not happy. I rescued a male cardinal from my cat, put it in a shoe box (Why is it always a shoe box?), and called the local humane society. "It doesn't seem hurt," I said, "it's not bleeding, but it's not dead. Could it be paralyzed with fear?" I knew it was alive by the brightness of its eye. "Put it in a protected place outdoors," said the voice at the other end of the phone, "and leave it alone." I went out to check on it every so often. The final time I checked, its eye was dull.

WINDOW CRASHERS

When birds see sky and trees reflected in your window, it looks like open space to them. If they keep crashing into a window, one thing you can do is break up the reflection by putting up a screen, nonreflective window coating, or flash tape on the *outside* of the window. (Cut-outs of falcons or owls and the like, supposed by some to warn birds off, do not really work.) You can also put a bird feeder close to or on the window to slow birds down.

Other options: plant trees or shrubs or install awnings to eliminate some or all of the reflection.

Note: Don't worry that birds' feet or eyes will freeze to metal parts of houses or feeders. Birds' feet have no sweat glands, and their reflexes are plenty fast enough to keep their eyes from touching metal.

DISCOURAGING UNINVITED GUESTS

If you come to my house as a guest, you have a right to expect that I'm not going to set my pet panther on you or invite the neighbors in to dine on your tender body parts. Though I support the survival of the fittest as staunchly as the next person, I think we owe our feathered guests the same courtesy. The most common and dangerous predators of the birds whose homes appear in *Beastly Abodes* are squirrels, cats, house sparrows and European starlings, and raccoons, in about that order.

No one seems to have come up with a surefire way to keep squirrels away from birds' eggs and fledglings, especially in exposed nests. Make sure the entry holes on your nest boxes are the right size for the birds you want to house, which is usually too small for squirrels. Fitting a circlet of metal around the entrance hole will keep squirrels from chewing their way in, but be sure no sharp edges remain that might injure the birds. If

your nest box is on a pole, you can wrap the pole with an eighteen-inch cylinder of sheet metal high enough so squirrels and cats can't leap over it, or you can mount a cone-shaped guard beneath the house, which should discourage raccoons as well as squirrels and cats.

To protect birds at your feeder from cats, the best strategy is to fit your own cats with elasticized collars and bells. Place bird feeders far away from likely jumping-off points in trees (although this makes birds at the feeder vulnerable to hawks). Place birdbaths off the ground and away from shrubbery where cats might hide.

To safeguard nesting birds and fledglings—and mice, in winter—you can buy a commercially available coon guard, a wire mesh tunnel that fits on the outside of nest boxes and deters cats, raccoons, and large birds from reaching inside. A piece of one-inch wood framing the entrance hole would also help. Both cats and raccoons avoid getting grease on their fur, so if you site your nest boxes on steel posts or concrete reinforcing rods, you can discourage these predators by smearing the posts with axle grease, available at hardware stores.

House sparrows and European starlings, which breed everywhere in the United States and southern Canada, not only compete for the nest boxes you put up but drive away native songbirds. Given the opportunity, house sparrows will kill a female songbird and her young in the nest, and they can invade any birdhouse with an entry hole of at least one and one-quarter inches. Starlings need an entrance hole larger than one and one-half inches.

Removing sparrow or starling nests as soon as you find them is a first step, but to protect nesting songbirds these two species need to be removed permanently from your property—these are the only two bird species unprotected by law that I know of. Contact your local Audubon group, ASPCA, or wildlife expert for advice if they are a problem for your invited bird guests.

GRAPEVINE NEST BASKET

DON DANIELS

As fairly careless nest builders themselves, mourning doves can be expected to welcome such efforts as this grapevine nest basket.

TOOLS AND MATERIALS

Pliers
Side cutters or clippers
Grapevine
Tie wire

WEAVING THE NEST BASKET

■ **STEP ONE** Wrap vines into five circles, 12", 10", 8", 6", and 4" across. Cut eight straight 10" pieces for bottom braces.

■ **STEP TWO** Wire two braces in a V shape, then wire their other ends to the inside of the 12" circle, as shown. Wire the other seven braces to the base and evenly spaced around the inside of the 12" circle.

■ **STEP THREE** Wire the other circles inside the braces, beginning with the 10" circle and working down to the 4" one.

■ **STEP FOUR** Add more vines, weaving them in and out of the braces to cover the cone. Weave a vine around the rim to cover the tops of the braces.

NEST BASKET LOCATION AND TIPS

The best location for your basket or cone is in the crotch of a horizontal tree limb at least six feet up in moderate shade. Some open space around it makes coming and going easier for the doves. Fasten it securely in place with roofing nails, staples, or wire (be sure no sharp points of wire remain sticking out). Be prepared to clean the basket out after the first nesting; the doves won't. (For notes on mourning doves, see page 56.)

"Two Peeps," by Linda Daniels

A DOVE TALE

TWO MOURNING DOVES FLEDGED IN A NEST OVER THE DANIELS' DRIVEWAY IN SEPTEMBER 1993, AND AS THE LEAVES *fell Don watched the hawks circling and worried about the exposed nest. Linda Daniels, who is a wildlife artist, took photographs of the nestlings just before a storm stripped away the last few leaves on the tree and most of the nest itself. The young doves hid in the bushes at the edge of the Daniels yard until the next day, when they headed south with their mother.*

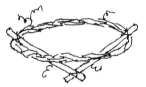

WIRE 2 BRACES
IN V SHAPE.

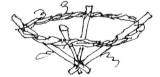

WIRE TO 12" CIRCLE.
ADD OTHER BRACES.

WIRE 10" CIRCLE TO BRACES—
8" CIRCLE, ETC.

ADD MORE VINES TO SURFACE—
COVER BRACES AROUND THE RIM.

"The doves nesting around my house need all the help they can get."
DON DANIELS, GRAPEVINE ARTIST

HONEYSUCKLE
NEST BASKETS

PAULA HEDRICK

Among the simplest and least expensive of the abodes to make, mourning dove nest baskets are among the most likely to draw birds—and to draw them over and over again. (Above, a variation.)

TOOLS AND MATERIALS

Clippers
15 pieces of #5 round reed, 12" long (or any round, sturdy pieces of vine)
Long weaving material (honeysuckle, English ivy, etc.)
1 rubber band
Water

WEAVING THE NEST BASKET

■ **STEP ONE** Soak the reed until it's pliable and easy to work with.

■ **STEP TWO** Bundle up seven pieces of the round reed, and hold them together with the rubber band about 1" from one end.

■ **STEP THREE** Stand over a table with the short end of the bundle facing up. As you push the bundle down, fan out the pieces of reed, or spokes, spacing them as evenly as possible. To hold them in this cone shape, lay books over two sides while you begin to weave.

■ **STEP FOUR** With a flexible piece of the long weaving material, staying as close to the rubber band as you can, weave over one reed and under the next, continuing in circles until you have woven a height of 2". This will hold the spokes in place.

■ **STEP FIVE** Insert one of the remaining eight spokes into the weave to the right of each existing spoke. You need an odd number of spokes, so on the last existing spoke, insert a new spoke on either side.

■ **STEP SIX** Continue weaving over one, under one, fanning out the spokes to keep an equal distance between them. Continue weaving until you have a circle about 12" across.

■ **STEP SEVEN** For the border, again soak the spokes (the part that you have not woven) until they are pliable.

■ **STEP EIGHT** Bend each spoke to the right, weaving it in front of the spoke to its right, then behind the next spoke, then tuck it in. On the last two spokes, insert the spokes into the rim where you started the pattern. Try to maintain the pattern as you do this.

■ **STEP NINE** When the reed is dry, clip the ends of each spoke in front of the third spoke to its right—this will hold the ends in place and prevent thcm from slipping out. (For location and mounting tips, see page 52.)

THE SIMPLEST
NEST BASKET OF ALL

YOU CAN MAKE A PERFECTLY SERVICEABLE NEST BASKET IN MINUTES WITH HARDWARE CLOTH, TIN CUTTERS, AND WIRE—THIS MAKES A GOOD ADULT-CHILD PROJECT. CUT a circle out of a twelve-by-twelve-inch piece of hardware cloth, Then cut out a pie-wedged shape (about one-twelfth of the circle) and join the cut edges with wire to make a cone. (Be sure no wire ends remain that might harm the birds.) Finally, wire your nest basket in the crotch of a tree limb at least six feet off the ground, with some shade.

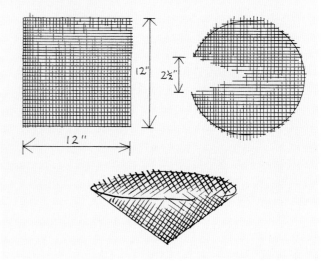

MOURNING DOVES

∎

Named for their plaintive call, mourning doves belong to the same family as domestic pigeons, are almost the same size, and waddle around in much the same way on their pinkish-orange feet. They are light brown, and adults have a black mark on their cheek. When startled, these birds lift off slowly with a great beating of wings and a series of alarmed-sounding coos. They are ground feeders and appreciate lots of seed. Even the young are on a seed-only diet after a week.

∎

You may be lucky enough to catch the male dove's courting display during breeding season, which lasts all spring and summer. With feathers spread and head nodding, he struts the ground in front of the female, or, wing tips held below his body, performs a spiraling, gliding aerial display above her.

∎

Among the most common backyard birds, mourning doves have more broods a year than any other North American bird—up to six. In this family of birds, both parents produce "crop milk," a protein- and fat-rich food that is all their young eat for the first week or so after hatching.

∎

The beauty of a mourning dove nest lies in its free-spirited nature. These doves usually pair off by late March and nest at least two or three times a summer, often moving into old robin or grackle nests or reusing their own. As gentle and domesticated as these birds seem, when the female builds her own nest she tends to throw it together in a few days with apparently careless abandon out of twigs collected by the male. She usually erects this frail structure on a horizontal branch anywhere from three to twenty feet up; sometimes she lines it with pine needles and grasses. Sometimes she lays her two white eggs right on the ground. (If more than two eggs or young birds appear in a nest, the extras have probably been dropped off by another female dove.) You can see the appeal a ready-made nest basket might have for this bird.

"Don't be intimidated by the use of honeysuckle in this project. You can use anything in your garden to weave with, providing it will bend almost in half without breaking. Most of the vine I use on my baskets is Virginia creeper from my woods. If it's green I have to boil it about three hours and then I can use it. I picked the gladioli leaves because of their interesting color—those you have to dry and resoak before you can weave with them. The main thing is to use your imagination and see what works. Sometimes your mistakes turn out to be the best things you make."

PAULA HEDRICK, BASKET MAKER

BARRED OWL NEST BOX

ROLF HOLMQUIST

Made almost entirely from found materials, this nest box combines elegance, art, function, and a woodsy look in a way that owls can't resist.

*"We had a screech owl roosting in this nest box this winter. About the hardware—
I gather a lot of found things from salvage yards, junkyards. When I see a neat thing,
I don't have a particular idea for it, I just throw it in a box. It's kind of a helter-skelter method."*

ROLF HOLMQUIST, WOOD ARTIST

TOOLS

Handsaw
Jigsaw
3/8" drill
1/4" drill bit
Screw bit/countersink (no. 8)
Phillips screwdriver
Tape measure

MATERIALS

Found wood
Barn wood (or other found wood) of any thickness:
Backboard: 6 x 34"
Back, entrance, & sides (2): 13 x 23" (4 total)
Roof: 16 x 17"
Floor: 12 x 12"

SUPPLIES

2-1/4" decking screws (no. 8)
Exterior wood glue

BUILDING THE BOX

■ **STEP ONE**   Cut all pieces as indicated. For the entrance, select one of the 13 x 23" pieces and mark lines at 4" and 11" from one end. Then mark lines 3" in from the sides between those two lines. Find a dish or pot lid with a 7" diameter and use it as a template to scribe a half-circle at the top of this marked area. Drill a 1/4" hole at one corner and cut along the lines to make a 7 x 7" entrance hole. (You can put the entrance hole on either the front or the side of the box.)

■ **STEP TWO**   Place the edge of the back piece against the inside of the entrance piece and mark four holes about 5" apart for drilling. Use a number 8 screw bit to drill into both pieces, then apply glue and fasten with decking screws. Repeat this procedure with the two side pieces, then assemble the box as a whole and fasten the two remaining corners in the same manner.

■ **STEP THREE**   Center the back of the box on the backboard and drill four mounting holes into the board, paired near the top and bottom of the box. Fasten with decking screws.

■ **STEP FOUR**   Measure the inside

opening at the lower end of the box to determine the exact dimensions of the floor. It should measure approximately 12 x 12". Cut the floor to the dimensions required and mount it 1/2" up from the box's lower edge by drilling holes through the sides and fastening it with decking screws. Use a 1/4" drill bit to bore six drain holes in the center of the floor.

■ **STEP FIVE**   Place the roof with one 16" edge flat against the backboard and an equal overhang at the adjacent edges. Apply glue to the box edges and use a number 8 screw bit to drill mounting holes through the roof. Fasten with decking screws.

■ **STEP SIX**   Attach found items and branches where desired.

■ **STEP SEVEN**   For mounting, drill 1/4" holes near the upper and lower ends of the backboard.

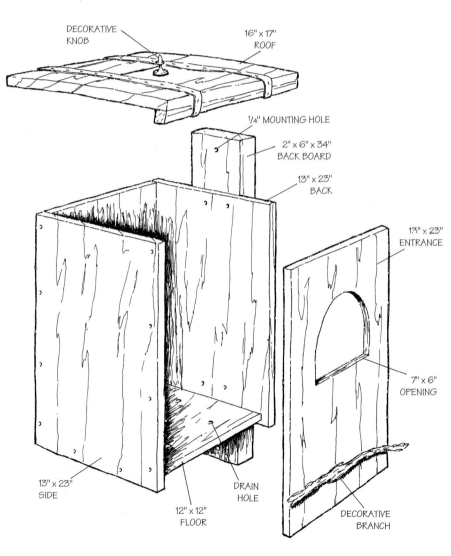

DECORATIVE KNOB

16" x 17" ROOF

1/4" MOUNTING HOLE

2" x 6" x 34" BACK BOARD

13" x 23" BACK

13" x 23" ENTRANCE

7" x 6" OPENING

13" x 23" SIDE

12" x 12" FLOOR

DRAIN HOLE

DECORATIVE BRANCH

BARRED OWLS

■

Long before robins show up or forsythia blooms, barred owls anticipate spring, often getting their nest-building under way in January. This means nest boxes intended for them need to be in place by Christmas.

■

In the nighttime woods—and sometimes during the day—you may mistake the cries of the barred owl for a barking dog. One observer of bird behavior, Lawrence Kilham, calls it "caterwauling" and says it is "one of the most thrilling vocalizations you are likely to hear in northern woods." The bird's normal repeated four-hoot call has been translated as sounding like "Who cooks for you, who cooks for you?"

■

Should you have binoculars handy or get close enough to check, these large (17-24") gray-brown, puffy-headed birds have big, round, brown eyes—the only other owl with brown eyes is the barn owl; the rest have yellow eyes. These owls are barred across the upper chest, streaked lengthwise on the belly, and spotted white on the back. They are year-round residents throughout eastern and midwestern North America and in parts of the far Northwest.

■

Barred owls often hunt during the day, feeding on small vertebrates (mice, squirrels, rabbits, snakes, and so on), moving through the air in silent, slow-flapping flight, often gliding.

■

To raise their once-a-year brood of two or three young, these birds prefer to nest in tree cavities in woodlands, wooded swamps, or river bottoms. Given the chance, they will reuse the same nest or nest box year after year.

BOX LOCATION AND TIPS

Put two to three inches of wood chips in the bottom of the nest box. The ideal site for the box is at least 20 feet up a tree with a relatively open trunk, if possible within 200 feet of water and at least 150 feet away from the nearest human residence—but not at the edge of a clearing. Young owls need perches fairly close to the nest, and adults appreciate an open flight path to the nest box—consider removing small trees that interrupt this path. To confound predators, you can wrap a sheet of tin or aluminum two feet wide around the tree about four feet up. If squirrels insist on moving in, you can discourage them by removing the nest box roof—they don't like topless boxes as well. It's best to clean the box out annually—just clear away the leaves and squirrels' debris.

Owl and Kestrel Box

Steve Mitchell

This versatile nest box will attract a number of species: American kestrels, eastern and western screech owls, northern saw-whet owls, and boreal owls, as well as grey, red, and fox squirrels. Who moves in will depend mainly on how big you make the entrance hole and where you site the box.

Tools

Handsaw
Jigsaw
3/8" drill
Screw bit/countersink (no. 6)
Drill bits (1/16", 1/4")
Phillips screwdriver
Flat-blade screwdriver
Tape measure
Cutting pliers
Compass

Materials

Western red cedar, 11/16" thick:
  Back: 9-1/8 x 22"
  Front: 9-1/8 x 16"
  Sides: 9-1/8 x 16" (2)
  Roof: 9-1/8 x 12"
  Floor: 7-3/4 x 9-1/8"

Supplies

1-1/2" decking screws (no. 6)
1" butt hinges (2)
4" copper wire (12 gauge)
1" brass roundhead screws (2, no. 6)
Exterior paint (brown, green)

Building the Box

- **Step One** Using a handsaw, cut all pieces.
- **Step Two** Drill a 1/4" vent hole through one corner of each side piece 2" from the long and the short edges. Drill four 1/4" drain holes in the floor piece, 2" from the short edges and 1-1/2" from the long edges.
- **Step Three** Mark a point 11-1/2" from one short edge of the front piece, centered in the face. Use a compass to draw a circle 3-1/4" in diameter around this point.

Drill a 1/4" hole at the edge of the marked circle and use a jigsaw to cut a 3-1/4" entrance hole in the wood.

- **Step Four** Mark a point 3" from one short edge of the back piece at both sides. Position the side pieces on edge along the sides with the lower corners at the 3" marks. Use a number 6 screw bit to drill three holes 7" apart along each side to secure the two pieces. Fasten the sides with decking screws. Then drill a 1/4" hole in the back, centered and 1" in from each short edge.
- **Step Five** Place the floor between the side pieces, flush with the lower edges and against the back piece. Use a number 6 screw bit to drill three holes 3" apart through the sides and into the edges of the floor. Fasten with decking screws.
- **Step Six** Position the front over the forward edges of the box, lower edge flush with the floor and with the entrance hole toward the top. Using a number 6 screw bit, drill three holes 7" apart along each side and one hole centered at the lower edge. Fasten with decking screws.
- **Step Seven** Center the roof against the upper part of the back piece. Position the two butt hinges 1" in from each side and mark the mounting holes. Drill 1/16" pilot holes at those points and fasten the hinges with the screws provided.
- **Step Eight** Mark a point 2-3/4" back from the face of the box and 1-1/2" down from the roof on one side. Use a number 6 screw bit to drill a pilot hole at this point and another directly above it in the edge of the roof. Drive a roundhead screw halfway into each hole. Then use pliers to loop the copper wire around the upper screw and bend hooks in the two ends to match the lower screw.
- **Step Nine** Sand the surfaces of the box and use the illustration to recreate the painted ivy pattern on the front, sides, and roof or create your own design.

Kestrel Box Location and Tips

These swallowlike falcons are among the first spring migrants; they begin looking for nesting cavities by February 1. If starlings live in your area, be prepared to check your kestrel box every week or ten days to remove starling eggs and nests. (Kestrel eggs are white to pinkish white, marked with browns or lavender; starling eggs are pale bluish or greenish white, marked with browns.) These spaced checks won't frighten the kestrels into abandoning the nest box.

*"We love the sound of screech owls at night in the woods around our house here in North Carolina.
I hope we can entice a pair to nest close by next year, once I get this box up."*

STEVE MITCHELL, WOODWORKER

Place nest boxes ten to thirty feet up on trees or posts in relatively open areas or in orchards and facing south or west, if possible. A sheet of tin or aluminum fastened around the tree under the box should prevent squirrels from moving in. Kestrels need grassy hunting habitat somewhere nearby.

Put two to three inches of wood chips (not sawdust) in the bottom of the nest box.

AMERICAN KESTRELS

Members of the streamlined and sleek falcon family, American kestrels often survey the world from power lines or dead trees throughout most of the Americas. We used to call them sparrow hawks, but in fact they're especially valuable because of the numbers of rodents and insects they eat. About the size of a jay (9-12"), they have reddish backs or tails and distinctive mustached black-and-white faces; males have blue-gray wings. The Peterson guides describe their call as "a rapid, high *klee klee klee* or *killy killy killy.*"

Kestrels nest and hunt in open country, cities, farmland, highway right-of-ways, deserts, and the edges of woods, and they are frequent users of nest boxes. (Evidently their numbers are limited by a lack of good nesting cavities, because local populations increase when nest boxes are provided.) In the South or where prey is plentiful, kestrels often use the same nest box for a second brood in the same season. They hover while hunting and hunt by day; if you're attracting birds to a feeder, you may (infrequently) attract kestrels to the birds.

SCREECH OWLS

Between them, eastern and western screech owls cover all of the continental United States except the area around the northern Rockies—year-round residents. Both species (they used to be one) are small (7-10") and have ear tufts. Both prefer to live in woodlands or wooded canyons, farm groves, or shade trees. They nest in tree cavities or hollow stumps, and the western variety also builds nests in building crevices or saguaro cactus cavities. Both have broods of four or five, with the male feeding the female for the twenty-six days or so it takes the eggs to hatch.

■

The eastern screech owl, as the Peterson field guides point out, is "our only small eastern owl with ear tufts." It is either gray or bright red-brown (the "only eared owl" that is). Its familiar, haunting night call is a mournful wail, a ghostly whinny that descends in pitch. Abundant in suburban and urban areas with mature trees, this small owl has recently declined in number, partly because the utility poles it sometimes uses for nesting have been painted with creosote, whose fumes poison birds.

■

Western screech owls are usually gray, occasionally brown. When nesting, they perform distraction displays if an intruder approaches—the adult owl will pretend to be injured, ill, or exhausted to tempt the intruder away from the nest. The closer to being able to fly the young are, the more elaborate and conspicuous these displays become, for the more the parents have invested.

■

Unlike their eastern relatives, who hunt at twilight as well as at night, western screech owls hunt only after dusk. (Owls "see" in the dark by relying on their highly developed sense of sound and by knowing the details of their territory—the height of favorite perches, for instance.)

SCREECH OWL BOX LOCATION AND TIPS

Screech owl boxes need to be located at least ten feet up on a tree or saguaro—or on a pole with a predator guard, to prevent squirrels from moving in (in fact, this box can be modified specifically for squirrels).

Put two or three inches of wood chips in the bottom of the box.

If starlings are a problem in your area, be on guard, as the three-inch entrance hole allows them entrance to the box.

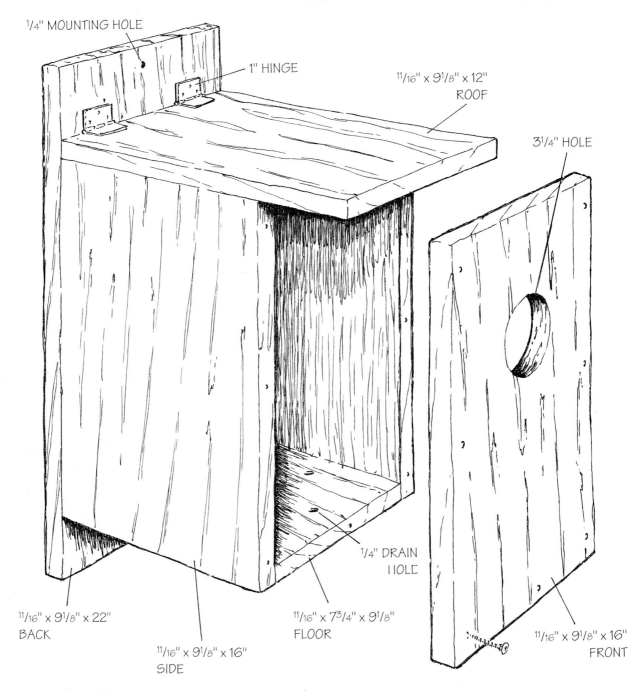

1/4" MOUNTING HOLE

1" HINGE

11/16" x 9 1/8" x 12"
ROOF

3 1/4" HOLE

11/16" x 9 1/8" x 22"
BACK

11/16" x 9 1/8" x 16"
SIDE

11/16" x 7 3/4" x 9 1/8"
FLOOR

1/4" DRAIN
HOLE

11/16" x 9 1/8" x 16"
FRONT

SAW-WHET OWL BOX LOCATION AND TIPS

Place saw-whet nest boxes fourteen to sixty feet off the ground in live mature trees. A nearby fresh water supply helps. Since a disturbed owl won't leave its box, you can check the box by tapping gently on the side—the owl will peep out of the entrance hole.

To protect the eggs, place two or three inches of wood chips in the bottom of the box.

BOREAL OWL BOX LOCATION AND TIPS

Boreal owls' nest boxes need to be from sixteen to twenty feet up in live hardwood trees, with a cleared space in front of the box and within 100 yards of conifers. If possible, according to Carroll Henderson in *Woodworking for Wildlife*, it is best to place the box "near a stand of lowland conifer habitat like a cedar swamp."

△ NORTHERN SAW-WHET OWLS

∎

Named for its distinctive call, reminiscent of a saw being sharpened, the saw-whet is only about eight inches tall, "a very tame little owl," according to the Peterson field guides. Its song is a one-note whistled repetition (some say "endless," others "incessant"), often over a hundred times a minute, with occasional key changes.

∎

Young saw-whets are chocolate brown with a conspicuous white V between their eyes and an ocher belly. Adults have brown-streaked bellies. These are shy birds. If disturbed at the nest, they retreat and refuse to leave the nest box.

∎

Cavity dwellers, saw-whets prefer to nest in forests, conifers, groves, wooded swamps, or bogs. They live year round in the northeastern United States, the Northwest, and higher elevations in the western states. (Teddy Roosevelt reported a saw-whet at the White House.)

∎

These nocturnal hunters, most active at dusk and just before dawn, eat mainly rodents.

BOREAL OWLS

∎

The small flat-headed, earless boreal owls ("very tame," according to the Peterson guides) resemble a slightly larger version of the northern saw-whet and live north of their territory in the boreal forests and bogs of the Western hemisphere, including the northern United States. In Europe this bird is called Tengmalm's owl.

∎

During courting, the female approaches the male, who then not only flies into a prospective nest hole and sings to her but offers her food from his cache in a tree fork or crevice. Males also feed nesting females from about a month before eggs are laid, for the twelve or so days of egg laying, and until about three weeks after the brood (usually of four to six young) hatches.

∎

In daylight boreal owls roost in barns or dense vegetation, hunting small mammals and other birds nocturnally. Like saw-whets and humans, they freeze their food and (unlike most humans) thaw it by incubating it as they would eggs.

∎

Boreal owls nest in abandoned woodpecker holes or natural cavities in mixed-wood and conifer forests (spruce, fir, white pine, jack pine, and cedar).

Northern Flicker Nest Box

MARK STROM

Depending on where you live, where you place the nest box, and the size of the entrance hole, this abode will serve not only flickers but hairy and red-headed woodpeckers and may also attract American kestrels, northern saw-whet owls, and screech owls.

TOOLS

Circular saw
Keyhole saw
3/8" drill
Drill bits (1/16", 1/4")
Screw bit/countersink (no. 8)
Phillips screwdriver
Tape measure
Protractor
Compass
Tack hammer
Pruning shears

MATERIALS

Willow twigs
Western red cedar, 3/4" thick and 7-1/4" wide:
  Back: 32"
  Sides: 24" (2)
  Bottom: 5-3/4"
  Top: 10-1/4"
  Front: 22-3/8"

SUPPLIES

1-1/4" decking screws (no. 8)
1" panel nails
1" butt hinges (2)
Linseed or tung oil

BUILDING THE BOX

■ **STEP ONE**   Use the protractor to measure and mark a 10° angle on one face end of each 24" side piece. Cut to this angle. The shorter edge should be about 22-3/8" long after the cut.

■ **STEP TWO**   Measure down 4-1/2" from the top end of the back piece and mark at the edges. Align the side pieces with the edges of the back piece, placing the upper angle points at the marks you just made. Using a number 8 screw bit, from the back side drill and countersink four holes per side to a depth of 1-1/4", spacing them 7-1/2" apart. Fasten the sides to the back with the decking screws. Drill a 1/4" mounting hole through the back 2" down from the top edge and centered.

■ **STEP THREE**   Measure 19" from one end of the front piece and 3-5/8" in from one edge at that point, and mark. Use a compass and this center point to scribe a 2-1/4"-diameter circle.

■ **STEP FOUR**   Drill a 1/4" hole at the edge of this circle, then use a keyhole saw to cut out the 2-1/4" entry hole.

■ **STEP FIVE**   Place the front piece with the hole toward the top onto the forward edges of the side pieces already attached. Align the top and bottom edges with the sides' corners and use a number 8 screw bit to drill 1-1/4"-deep countersunk holes 7" apart, four to a side. Fasten the front with decking screws.

■ **STEP SIX**   Measure and cut a 10° angle into the forward and rear edges of the top. These angles should be parallel to one another and to the front and rear faces of the box. Center the top on the box and use the number 8 screw bit to drill a 1-1/4"-deep countersunk hole in each corner. Fasten with decking screws.

■ **STEP SEVEN**   Drill four 1/4" holes near the edges of the bottom piece. Slip the bottom into place in the box and trim the edges if necessary for fit. Position the hinges 1" in from the side edges and use the 1/16" bit and the hinge screws provided to fasten the hinges to the rear of the box. Drill a countersunk hole 1-1/4" deep through the front and into the bottom piece; a decking screw will hold the bottom in place and can be removed for cleaning at the end of the nesting season.

■ **STEP EIGHT**   With pruning shears, cut appropriate lengths of willow or other pliable 3/8-1/2" twigs to cover the cedar box. It's best to use ribbed panel nails to fasten twigs at the edges first, then fill in each surface between as needed. Leave the mounting hole at the top and screw head latch at the bottom accessible. You can finish the twig surface with boiled linseed or tung oil if it's applied at least a month in advance of nesting season.

"For this twig pattern, you could use just about any kind of green, flexible wood. Maple would work well. After every nesting season, if you put some kind of water sealer or weather sealant on the outside of this box, it'll last a lot longer."

MARK STROM, WOOD SCULPTOR

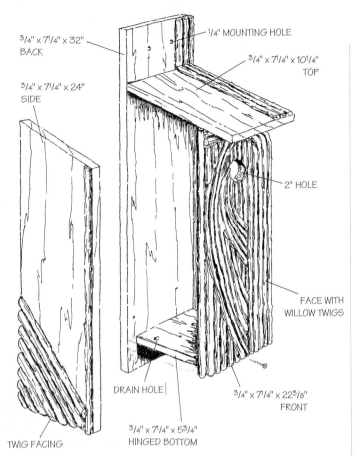

3/4" x 7 1/4" x 32"
BACK

1/4" MOUNTING HOLE

3/4" x 7 1/4" x 10 1/4"
TOP

3/4" x 7 1/4" x 24"
SIDE

2" HOLE

FACE WITH
WILLOW TWIGS

DRAIN HOLE

3/4" x 7 1/4" x 22 3/8"
FRONT

TWIG FACING

3/4" x 7 1/4" x 5 3/4"
HINGED BOTTOM

NEST BOX LOCATION AND TIPS

One of the secrets to attracting flickers to your nest box is to fill the box full of sawdust before April 1. Just as if the box were a dead tree with soft heartwood, the bird will start excavating sawdust at the entrance hole and keep tossing it out until it's made the cavity it wants.

Squirrels, kestrels, screech owls, and northern saw-whet owls have been known to nest in abandoned flicker holes, so if any of these species occur in your area, you may find them in your flicker nest box until you clean it and fill it back up with sawdust. Flickers will often return to the same nesting site year after year.

Entrance holes for red-headed woodpeckers should be two inches in diameter, for hairy woodpeckers, one and five-eighths inches. For woodpeckers, place the box near the edge of woodland clearings that have a nearby water source and, as for flickers, fill it with sawdust.

For flickers, place the box four to six feet high on a post beside a field or pasture or in an orchard or woodlot.

RED-HEADED WOODPECKERS

■

The first time I saw a red-headed woodpecker I found myself repeating softly, "Wow. Wow. Wow." The entire head of this strikingly marked bird is a deep scarlet, as if it were wearing a smooth red hood. Between a cardinal and robin in size (8-1/2–9-1/2"), it has a solid black back, white rump and breast, and black wings with large square white patches. It breeds mainly east of the Rockies, from southern Canada to the Gulf, in farm country, groves, and shade trees in towns.

■

These birds usually produce four or five white eggs in each of their one or two broods a season. The parents take turns sitting on the eggs, which hatch in twelve or thirteen days; the young fly in about a month. Red-headed woodpeckers store food when it is abundantly available, breaking up insects, acorns, and beechnuts to cache them in natural cavities.

■

Red-headed woodpecker survival has been of special concern for some years. Young reared in creosote-coated utility poles die, and there is a good deal of competition for these woodpeckers' preferred nesting cavities in dead trees, fences, and other poles. In areas with sparse nest sites and with good supplies of insects for food, woodpecker nest boxes are a boon to the species.

NORTHERN FLICKERS

■

If you live in the continental United States, you probably have flickers for neighbors. Since they are one of the most common yard-nesting species, your chances of attracting them to a nest box are high. Although flickers seldom come to feeders, they nest almost anywhere—open forests, woodlots, farms, groves, towns, suburbs, deserts— and in almost anything—cavities in poles and posts, saguaros, houses, earthen banks, haystacks, and boxes.

■

These large (12-14") woodpeckers have barred brown backs, a black patch across the chest like a short bib, and in flight a white rump. Unlike most woodpeckers, they often hop awkwardly along the ground, pecking at ants. They come in three basic types: red-shafted in the West, yellow-shafted in the North and East, and gilded in the southeastern deserts.

■

Flickers go through elaborate noisy rituals during courtship—members of a facing pair call, drum their feet, flash their wings and tails, bob their heads. Their song is a loud "wick-wick-wick-wick-wick" or squeaky "flicka, flicka, flicka."

■

Flicker eggs take only eleven to fourteen days to hatch, and the young fly within another month. The average clutch is from five to eight eggs.

HAIRY WOODPECKERS

The hairy woodpecker is an exaggerated and shyer version of the downy woodpecker (see the downy's description on page 96)—slightly larger and with a noticeably longer bill. Its breeding range runs from Alaska to Panama, and it prefers to breed in forests and woodlands, wooded swamps, orchards, and towns and parks with plenty of trees. Hairys eat mostly insects and may hoard them in small caches against the winter, when they also eat acorns, hazelnuts, and beechnuts.

■

These woodpeckers pair up in winter. During courtship, both males and females drum, striking their bills against hollow or dry branches, metal gutters, drainpipes, and other satisfying tympanylike instru-

ments. Males also freeze-pose, and females make fluttering flights to attract males.

■

The male usually chooses the nest cavity, and both parents incubate the eggs (white, usually four), the male at night, the female by day. Eggs hatch in about two weeks, and the young fledge in about a month, although the parents continue to care for the fledglings for several more weeks.

■

As with some other woodpeckers, the decline of hairys has been widely reported—house sparrows and starlings, more aggressive birds, often take over their nest cavities, and the displaced hairys frequently don't have time in the same season to produce another brood.

RUSTIC NESTING SHELF

BOBBY HANSSON

This rustic design is a proven barn swallow favorite. It's simple, inexpensive, and intended for short-term use—a year or two. Since these swallows often nest in loose colonies, it's a good idea to put up two or three shelves together. (Be aware that your shelf may also attract American robins or eastern phoebes.)

TOOLS AND MATERIALS

Saw
Hammer
Drywall screws or finishing nails
Plywood scraps, about 7 x 8" for floor, 8 x 8-1/2" for roof
A three-pronged branch (here, cherry), the prongs about 6" long

BUILDING THE SHELF

■ **STEP ONE**   Cut the tops of the three prongs at a slight angle, so rain will run off the slanted roof. To be sure you cut them so that the roof will fit solidly on them, hold the bottom of the branch in water at about the angle you want, in a way that the top of the water leaves a watermark near the tops of the prongs. Then saw at those marks.

■ **STEP TWO**   For the roof, lay the branch flat on a table (as if the table were the side of the house where the shelf will hang). Then position the larger piece of plywood, the roof, on top of the branch, mark a line about 1" beyond the prongs, and saw.

■ **STEP THREE**   For the floor, use a piece of thin cardboard to make a template, or pattern, that fits snugly between the prongs about 4-5" below the roof. Draw this pattern on the other piece of plywood and saw. (It may be easier to saw the pattern in several pieces and glue or wedge them together to fit inside the prongs.)

BARN SWALLOWS

A remarkable thing about barn swallows is the distance they migrate—up to 7,000 miles a year. The only true swallow-tailed swallow, with its deeply forked tail, the barn swallow (6-7-3/4") glides and swoops throughout most of North America and begins nesting in April. Blue-black above, cinnamon-buff below, these birds attach their cup-shaped mud nests to ledges and walls of buildings, usually under roofs of some kind, often barns—thus the name. They favor open or partly open land, fields, marshes, farms, and lakes.

■

Like all members of the swallow family, barn swallows capture their food in flight; they also drink and bathe on the wing, dipping to the surface of ponds or rivers.

■

Barn swallows frequently return to the same nesting site year after year, sometimes to the same nest and same mate. They have two broods a year, and you will often see more than two barn swallows at one nest, on occasion helping to feed the nestlings— the visitors are the young from the previous year or from that year's earlier clutch, helping their parents. After fledging, newborn barn swallows also return to the nest for a few days to roost.

"Barn swallows insisted on building nests under my neighbors' porch roof. Their daughter loved to watch them fly and catch bugs, but her father was tired of bird droppings on the porch and was getting cranky about their swooping down to defend their nest. I made a shelf like this and nailed it to the side of the house near the birds' niche from the year before, and they moved in. Now everyone's happy."

BOBBY HANSSON, DESIGNER

EASTERN PHOEBES

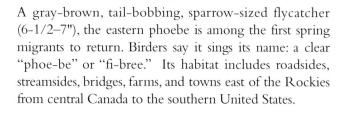

A gray-brown, tail-bobbing, sparrow-sized flycatcher (6-1/2–7"), the eastern phoebe is among the first spring migrants to return. Birders say it sings its name: a clear "phoe-be" or "fi-bree." Its habitat includes roadsides, streamsides, bridges, farms, and towns east of the Rockies from central Canada to the southern United States.

Eastern phoebes have two broods a summer and will tend to use the same nest for both if the first brood was

successful. They often renovate old nests, occasionally those of barn swallows, who use the same cup-shaped design. Their nests are delicately woven creations of moss and plant fibers lined with feathers, hair, and grass.

Like most flycatchers, phoebes often sit motionless on exposed branches from which they make short sallies to snap up insects, returning to the same perch—they are particularly easy to spot on branches that overhang water.

The apparent decline of eastern phoebes in parts of the East and Midwest is cause for concern. One culprit may be the brown-headed cowbird, who regularly lays its eggs in the nests of 220 other species, eastern phoebes included. When this occurs, phoebes may build a new nest floor over the cowbird eggs or may abandon the nest—often, they raise the cowbird young with their own. Building a new nest or new nest floor results in fewer eggs in the next clutch, and rearing the intruder's young nearly always means less food and care for the smaller phoebe young. Phoebe eggs are white, about 0.8"; the last laid may have small brown spots. Brown-headed cowbirds lay white to grayish white eggs, marked with browns, of about the same size; bronzed cowbirds (which breed only in the arid Southwest and parasitize 77 species) lay slightly larger pale bluish-green eggs.

■ **STEP FOUR** Use three screws or nails to attach the roof to the prongs (predrill and use drywall screws if you're afraid the wood will split).

SHELF LOCATION AND TIPS

Attach the shelf to the wall of a building at least seven feet off the ground where predators can't get at it—you may have better luck attracting phoebes to your shelf if you live near water. Placing the shelf under an eave provides more protection for the birds and may draw them more readily. Because swallows defend their nests against people passing nearby, it's a good idea to locate shelves for them at least ten to twenty feet from a doorway or other highly traveled route.

GOURD HOUSES FOR SWALLOWS

ELAINE KNOLL, GLADYS SMITH,
AND GEORGE KNOLL

Foresters' practice of removing standing dead trees has meant far fewer natural nesting sites available for both violet-green and tree swallows. Like their relatives the purple martins, tree swallows are somewhat colonial—you can hang two or three gourds together for them on a post or dead tree.

"If I can paint one of these, anyone can."
GLADYS SMITH, DESIGNER

MAKING THE HOUSE

- **STEP ONE** Soak the gourd in a solution of 1/4 cup bleach to a gallon of water for half an hour. Wearing rubber gloves, scrub with pot scrubber or steel wool pad. Remove every bit of dirt, mold, and mildew from the gourd, or the decorative paint will eventually flake off. Rinse, towel dry, then air dry for half an hour.

- **STEP TWO** To allow for hanging the gourd, drill or carve a 5/16" hole about an inch down from the top.

- **STEP THREE** Mark the entry hole 4-6" above the gourd bottom, if possible. You may want to hang the gourd up to find the best angle and position for it. Mark the measurements for the entry hole with a pencil: the ideal entry hole for tree swallows is 1-1/2" across and 2-3/8" high. For violet-green swallows, make an oval or diamond-shaped entry hole 3-1/2" wide and 7/8" high.

- **STEP FOUR** You may choose to drill a 5/16" starting hole in the middle of the entry hole. A flexible shaft grinder with a cylindrical carbide burr does a nice job of grinding out the hole, but you can also use a good, sharp utility knife.

- **STEP FIVE** Drill or carve three or four small drainage holes—about 5/16" in the bottom of the gourd, beginning with one at the lowest spot and spacing the others around it.

- **STEP SIX** Completely clean out the insides of the gourd. (A dust mask will keep the dried pulp dust out of your mouth.)

- **STEP SEVEN** Treat the gourd with a preservative as described in "Tips for Gourd Birdhouses," page 105.

- **STEP EIGHT** If the gourd has a smooth, even natural color, you don't need a base coat. Otherwise, to create an even background, dab on white outdoor primer paint with a sponge. Paint all cut edges, but be

TOOLS

Drill or sharp utility knife
Flexible shaft grinder with cylindrical carbide burr (optional)
Note: Please read "Tips for Gourd Birdhouses" on page 104 for important additional directions..

MATERIALS AND SUPPLIES

Dried gourd, 9" diameter
Household bleach
Rubber gloves
Pot scrubber or steel wool pad
Pencil
Ruler
Clean sponge for painting
White outdoor primer paint
Exterior latex paint (for other than natural background)
Acrylic paints
High-gloss spar urethane

"A friend hung one of our gourds on her porch and a bird moved in the next day, so we know they work. Making these shouldn't be difficult for anyone, even a beginner. They can improvise their own design, their own colors and flowers. But it's important to coat the finished gourd with the urethane to protect it."

ELAINE KNOLL, DESIGNER

TREE SWALLOWS AND VIOLET-GREEN SWALLOWS

All eighty-one species of the swallow family like to perch in long rows on wires. In flight, all are graceful gliders rather than wing flappers. Luckily for us, of the eight species in the United States, three will nest in gourds and birdhouses: tree swallows, violet-green swallows, and purple martins (barn swallows will use nesting shelves).

The two-toned tree swallow is a solid, almost iridescent, dark green/blue/black above, all white below, and slightly smaller than a house sparrow, five to six inches. They breed throughout the northern and western United States along the edges of woodlands and in open country, often near water, and winter in Florida and south. Very similar in size and coloring, the violet-green swallow has a greener back and white patches that almost meet across the rump. (The dark violet patches at nape and rump are often hard to spot.) These swallows nest in the western United States from central Alaska south to Mexico, in a variety of habitat from mountains to canyons to cities.

Tree swallows fly complex patterns in courtship, and early rising humans can enjoy the predawn flight songs of violet-green swallows, which may also be related to courtship. Both species produce one brood of four to six young a year; eggs hatch in fourteen to sixteen days, and the young can fly about three weeks later. Both species are also voracious insect eaters, a boon to gardeners, sunbathers, and other people with skin.

Nest-building tree swallows will take feathers from your upraised hand if they need them, especially on breezy days, according to Alfred G. Martin, the author of *Hand-Taming Wild Birds at the Feeder.*

sure no paint gets inside the gourd and keep the drainage holes free of clogs.

■ **STEP NINE** To create a white or color background, sponge one or two coats of exterior latex paint over the primer. Again, be extremely careful not to let any paint drip into the gourd or clog the drainage holes. Allow the paint to dry thoroughly.

■ **STEP TEN** Trace your design on the gourd and paint with acrylic paints. Erase all tracing lines when dry. Finish with a good coat of high-gloss spar urethane, again taking care not to clog the drainage holes or allow any finish inside the gourd.

GOURD LOCATION AND TIPS

Among the earliest spring migrants, tree and violet-green swallows begin arriving at their breeding territories in late February and early March (by May in the farther north areas)—it's best to hang the gourd before they arrive, and to face the entrance hole away from prevailing winds. Gourds for tree swallows need to be about four to five feet off the ground, preferably near a large water source (marsh, pond, river, etc.). Violet-green swallows nest from ten to fifteen feet up; they may find a gourd hung under the eave of a house especially attractive. So that your tenants don't freeze or roast, consider that darker gourds will absorb heat, light-colored gourds will reflect it.

"When I'm drilling gourds, I use a piece of hollowed-out foam to help hold the gourd in position on the drill press table. If you use a hand drill, you'll need someone to hold the gourd down for you or you'll quickly find out how easily a gourd will break if you drop it. When you clean the gourd out, wear a dust mask. The dried pulp is very dusty, and without a mask you will end up tasting it all day. "

GEORGE KNOLL, WOODWORKER

GOURD MARTIN HOUSES

LEW APPLEBAUM

The purple martin is the only bird species in eastern North America that depends entirely on humans for nest sites. You can double your chances of attracting martins by offering them both houses and gourds, according to the Purple Martin Conservation Association. Painted and preserved gourds may last through thirty martin seasons.

TOOLS

Electric drill and 1/4" bit
#2 hole saw mandrel and hole saw or short saw blade
Long-handled spoon
Note: Please read "Tips for Gourd Birdhouses" on page 104 for important additional directions. As with other gourd projects, electric tools are not essential; holes can be cut with hand drills, saw blades, or sharp utility knives.

MATERIALS AND SUPPLIES

5 gourds (or number desired), minimum 7-8" diameter
    and at least 1/4" thick
Steel wool
Plastic-coated copper wire
1 can spar varnish or white, polyurethane, high-gloss
    enamel
1 old bicycle wheel
1 pole, minimum 12'

MAKING THE HOUSE
(FOR EACH GOURD)

■ **STEP ONE** Soak the gourd for about 15 minutes in hot, soapy water and scrub off all dirt and mold with steel wool. Rinse well and allow to dry completely (but see step 2).

■ **STEP TWO** The entry hole needs to be perpendicular to the vertical axis of the gourd when suspended—anywhere along the outer part of the curve. Cut the hole with a hole saw or short saw blade to a diameter of between 1-3/4" and 2-1/8". (If you use a saw blade, cut the gourd while it's still damp from washing.)

■ **STEP THREE** With the gourd suspended from your fingers, mark the lowest point on the bottom. Around this point drill seven 5/16" drainage holes, spaced about 2" apart.

■ **STEP FOUR** Drill two sets of 5/16" hanging holes about 2" down from the top of the neck (you'll use only one set, depending on how you want to the gourd to swing).

■ **STEP FIVE** If the shape of the gourd allows, drill four 1/2" ventilation holes on the neck, about 2" below these hanging holes.

■ **STEP SIX** Clean out the inside of the gourd with a long-handled metal spoon or screwdriver. If it's stubborn, soak it in water for a few hours to soften the debris.

■ **STEP SEVEN** After the gourd has dried for at least 48 hours, sand lightly so that paint will stick. Martins like white houses; you increase the attracting power of your gourds if you give them two coats of white, polyurethane, high-gloss enamel (latex paint peels sooner). Paint all cut edges, but not the inside of the gourd. *Take care not to clog the drainage holes,* or nestlings may drown.

■ **STEP EIGHT** Attach gourds to the bicycle wheel with plastic-coated copper wire in a way that they swing but don't twist, and spaced so they can't bump each other. Attach wheel to pole; for easier management, rig a pulley system for raising and lowering the wheel, if possible.

GOURD LOCATION AND TIPS

You can hang as many gourds as you like in your yard, at any height from ten to twenty feet. By attaching each hanging wire to its support on both sides of the gourd's neck, a gourd will swing but not twist in the wind. (Don't use bare wire—it will cut right through the gourd.) Be sure to space the gourds so they don't bump into each other.

Hang gourds beginning in early January in the South to late May or early June in the North. By mid-September, take gourds down for the winter. Don't let any other birds live in your martin gourds! For more siting and housing tips, see page 84.

"I used bird house and Indonesian bottle gourds for this collection, but any hard-shell gourds will work. The larger the better, up to thirteen inches around. If they're too small, the nestlings get crowded and might get pushed out."
LEW APPLEBAUM, DESIGNER

PURPLE MARTINS

Most people who enjoy hosting birds eventually explore the possibilities of housing purple martins. Beyond the attractiveness of martin houses themselves, the birds' behavior is fun to watch; they are graceful flyers (members of the swallow family); their song is beautiful; they eat enormous quantities of insects; and they return to the same sites year after year, often on about the same date each spring. Once you attract them, you've probably got them for life.

■

Martins are the largest North American swallow (7-1/2–8-1/2"); males are our only dark-bellied swallow, blue-black all over; females and young males have light grayish bellies and throats.

■

Their breeding range stretches across the eastern United States to a line running from central North Dakota south through Texas, plus a thin strip on the west coast of California and southern Oregon and a finger that reaches into Arizona and New Mexico. Purple martin habitat includes towns, farms, and open country, often near water—in Arizona, they nest in saguaros.

■

The forestry practice of removing standing dead trees contributed to the decline of purple martins in many areas; while they are not on the endangered list, there is cause for concern. Martins often drink and bathe on the wing, and they catch all of their food in flight; they are thus unusually vulnerable to weather conditions that affect insect numbers and begin to die of starvation after four or five days of poor weather. In many areas of the United States, the survival of the species depends on our providing and monitoring plenty of good nest sites.

GROWING YOUR OWN BIRDHOUSES

THE SECRET TO GROWING GOURDS FOR CRAFT PROJECTS WOULD SEEM TO BE PATIENCE. FOR INSTANCE, LAGENARIAS ARE PERFECT FOR BIRDHOUSES BUT, DEPENDING ON their size, take three months to a year to dry, or cure.

Lagenarias are named for their shape—bottle gourds, penguins or powder horns, swans, and balls are among the shapes that work well for birdhouses. They dry to a thin, solid waterproof shell and can be grown in temperate climates.

You can find gourd seeds through the American Gourd Society and major seed companies. Because gourds require a long growing season, in northern states it's a good idea to start seeds early in pots filled with good potting soil, well watered. Cover

with half an inch of soil and press down. Put the pot in a plastic bag and let seeds germinate in a warm place—two to five weeks. When a seedling appears, move the plant to a warm, sunny window and water as needed until you can transplant it outdoors.

Gourd vines grow about as fast as Jack's beanstalk, and those of large species can grow up to four stories high, given something to climb. Once gourds appear on the plant, you can alter their shape by tying parts of them with cloth or rope or by placing them in bottles or other containers.

For helpful information on gourds: American Gourd Society, P.O. Box 274-P, Mt. Gilead, Ohio 43338.

Purple Martin House

Mark Strom

You might not build a martin house this handsome in a weekend, but the results—as you can see—make the time and care worthwhile. It's the kind of birdhouse people driving by slow down to look at; you might be tempted to put up tiny decorations for winter holidays.

Tools

Table saw
Jigsaw
3/8" drill
Screw bit/countersink (no. 6)
Drill bits (1/8", 1/2", 5/16")
2-1/4" hole saw
Phillips screwdriver
Finishing hammer
Nail set
Staple gun
Tape measure
Try square

Materials

Exterior plywood, 1/4" thick:
  Floor: 25 x 25"
  Ceiling: 24 x 25"
  Partitions: 6 x 18-3/4" (4)
       6 x 22-3/4" (4)
  Roof panels: 14-1/8 x 25" (2)
  Roof gables: 6 x 24" (6)
Pine, 3/4" thick:
  Base: 7-1/4 x 7-1/4"
  Post mount: 3-1/2 x 3-1/2" (2)
       3-1/2 x 5" (2)
1" pine ripped from dimensional stock:
  Frame: 1-1/2 x 25" (2)
       1-1/2 x 23" (3)
  Frame braces: 1-1/2 x 11" (2)
  Rail posts: 1 x 2-1/2" (4)
  Floor and roof corner blocks: 1 x 2" (8)
1/2" dowel:
  Ridge molding: 25"
  Roof dowels: 29", 12" (1 each)
  Dowel rails: 24" (8)
4 x 4" cedar post, 10–18' long

"This is a project for people who like to measure and fit things. I'm a wood carver, and I like to eyeball things; you can't eyeball a martin house. You can adapt the measurements for thicker wood—although using plywood saves you a lot of money."

MARK STROM, WOOD SCULPTOR

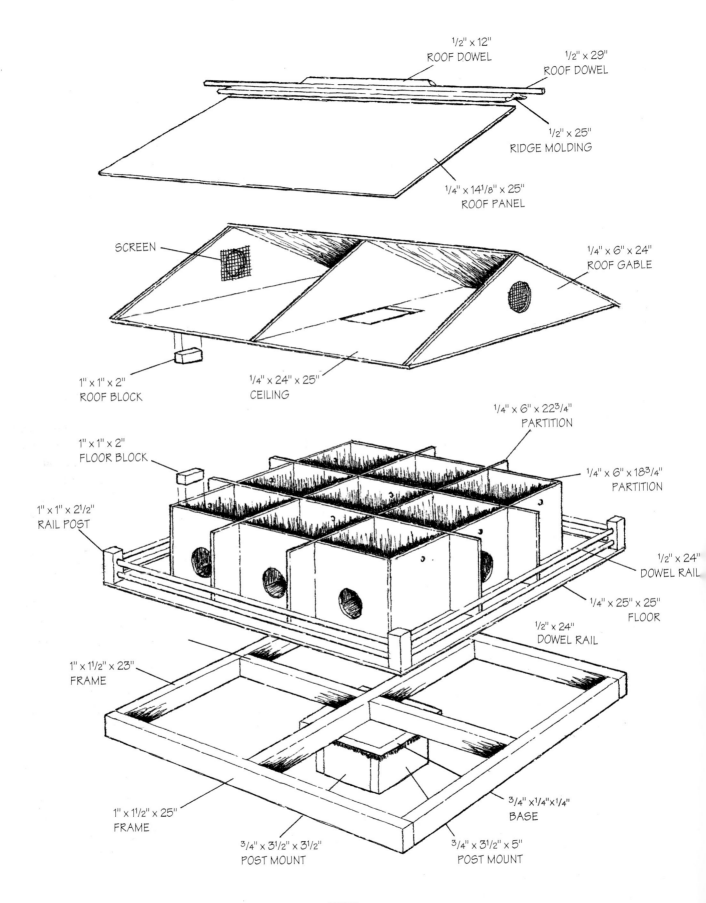

1/2" x 12"
ROOF DOWEL

1/2" x 29"
ROOF DOWEL

1/2" x 25"
RIDGE MOLDING

1/4" x 14 1/8" x 25"
ROOF PANEL

SCREEN

1/4" x 6" x 24"
ROOF GABLE

1" x 1" x 2"
ROOF BLOCK

1/4" x 24" x 25"
CEILING

1" x 1" x 2"
FLOOR BLOCK

1/4" x 6" x 22 3/4"
PARTITION

1/4" x 6" x 18 3/4"
PARTITION

1" x 1" x 2 1/2"
RAIL POST

1/2" x 24"
DOWEL RAIL

1/4" x 25" x 25"
FLOOR

1/2" x 24"
DOWEL RAIL

1" x 1 1/2" x 23"
FRAME

1" x 1 1/2" x 25"
FRAME

3/4" x 1/4" x 1/4"
BASE

3/4" x 3 1/2" x 3 1/2"
POST MOUNT

3/4" x 3 1/2" x 5"
POST MOUNT

SUPPLIES

3/4" decking screws (no. 6)
1-1/2" decking screws (no. 8)
3/4" brads (18 gauge)
1-1/4" brads (16 gauge)
1" finish nails
2" finish nails
3/8" staples
6 x 6" wire screen
Exterior wood glue
Exterior paint (white; trim color of your choice)

BUILDING THE HOUSE

Note: Sand all pieces before assembling.

■ **STEP ONE** Cut out the plywood floor piece. Cut the seven frame pieces. Glue and nail the two 25" frame sections beneath opposite edges of the plywood floor, narrow edge down, using 3/4" brads.

■ **STEP TWO** Glue and nail the three 23" frame pieces at right angles between the two already in place, with an 11" space between each. Locate the center of the midframe piece and fasten the remaining two 11" frame pieces at this point. Then set 2" finish nails into the corners and cross-braces to secure the frame.

■ **STEP THREE** Cut the four 18-3/4" partitions. On two pieces only, measure 3", 9-1/4", and 15-1/2" from one end and mark; then measure 2-1/8" from one edge and mark at each point. On the remaining two pieces, measure in 9-3/8" from one end and mark; then measure 2-1/8" from one edge and mark at those spots. Use a 2-1/4" hole saw to drill the eight entrance openings at the marked points.

■ **STEP FOUR** On all four pieces, measure in 6" from each end and 3" from the top edge (the one furthest from the hole). At these points, measure 1/8" to either side and mark, using a try square. Cut the eight 1/4 x 3" slots from the top edge with a jigsaw.

■ **STEP FIVE** Cut the four 22-3/4" partitions. On two pieces, measure in 2" and 2-1/4" from each end and mark; then measure in 7-3/4" and 8" and mark. Strike a line lengthwise down the center of each partition, then use a try square to extend the marks—the center pair toward one edge and the outer pair toward the opposite edge. On the remaining two pieces, measure in 1-3/4" and 2" from each end and mark; then measure in 7-7/8" and 8-1/8" and mark. Strike a line down the center as before, then use a try square to

extend the marks all toward the same edge. Cut the sixteen 1/4 x 3" slots with a jigsaw.

■ **STEP SIX** Drill a 5/16" vent hole centered 1" from the unslotted edge of the two 22-3/4" partitions with the slots on one side. Drill three 5/16" vent holes centered 6-3/8" apart and 1" from the top edge of the two 18-3/4" partitions with single entrance holes.

■ **STEP SEVEN** Use glue and 3/4" brads to fasten the ends of the two single-entrance partitions to the edges of the two triple-entrance partitions. All the slots should be facing in the same direction. Slip the four 22-3/4" partitions into the cut slots.

■ **STEP EIGHT** Cut the eight 2" floor and roof blocks. Center the partition assembly on the surface of the floor. Mark inside the four corners and glue one block at each. Fasten with 1-1/4" brads.

■ **STEP NINE** Cut the ceiling panel. Center the partition assembly on the ceiling and repeat the marking and fastening procedure for the remaining four blocks. Measure out a 5 x 5" ventilation square in the center of the ceiling panel and cut it out with a jigsaw.

■ **STEP TEN** Cut the six 6 x 24" roof gables. Glue and staple the pieces together in pairs. Mark the center on one edge of each assembly, then draw diagonals from those points to the bottom corners. Cut on the lines to make three roof gables. Drill a 2-1/4" hole in the center of two of these. Staple a 3 x 6" wire screen over each of these openings.

■ **STEP ELEVEN** Glue and nail the vented gables flush to the 24" ends of the ceiling panel using 3/4" brads. Center and fasten the third gable in the same way.

■ **STEP TWELVE** Cut the two roof panels. Fasten them to the gables using glue and 3/4" brads. Cut a 25" length of cove molding, and 12" and 29" lengths of 1/2" dowel. Predrill all holes with an 1/8" bit and fasten the molding to the roof ridge using glue and 3/4" brads. Glue and nail the longer dowel to the top of the molding using 1-1/4" brads. Glue and nail the short dowel to the top of the dowel just fastened using 1-1/4" brads.

■ **STEP THIRTEEN** Cut the four 2-1/2" rail posts. Measure down 3/4" and 1-7/8" from one end of each and mark on two adjoining faces. Drill 1/2" holes 3/8" deep at all marks. Cut the eight 24" dowel rails. Fasten one post to the floor using glue and a 2" nail set through a predrilled hole. Insert two rails and fasten the second post; continue until all rails and posts are fastened.

- **STEP FOURTEEN** Place the partition assembly on top of the floor and set 3/4" brads into the floor blocks at the corners. Place the roof assembly on top of the partitions and secure it with four 3/4" screws fastened into the roof blocks.
- **STEP FIFTEEN** To make the socket into which the mounting pole will fit, cut the 3-1/2" and 5" post mounts. Use glue and 2" finish nails to butt the longer pieces against the ends of the shorter ones. Glue and nail the completed mount to the 7-1/4" base. Then glue and nail the entire assembly to the center of the framing beneath the floor. Use 2" finish nails.
- **STEP SIXTEEN** To protect the wood (and to attract martins), paint the house with several coats of white exterior paint and the trim with exterior paint in your choice of colors, using the photo as a guide.
- **STEP SEVENTEEN** Mount the house on the 4 x 4" cedar post with shelf brackets or number 8 decking screws.

HOUSE LOCATION AND TIPS

- Martins bond with their established nesting sites. This is good news in that, once they have nested in your yard, they will probably be back. The bad news is that if any other bird nests in the house before a martin has nested there, that house or gourd will rarely attract a martin. This means checking the housing for alien nests and pulling them out (when martins are nesting); before martins arrive, you can plug entrance holes with paper cups to repel invaders.

- Martins like living near people—place your house or gourds in the center of the most open spot available, thirty to a hundred feet from human housing. The farther from trees the better, and no trees taller than the martin housing within at least forty feet of it. (Southern martins are less fussy—they'll nest within fifteen feet of trees.) Martins need a level flight path to and from their housing in several directions. This open space is a *critical* requirement.

- Put up a predator pole guard, and keep the pole clear of vines and shrubs, which martins seem to know make their homes more accessible to predators.

- Ideally, martin houses and gourds need to be checked weekly for parasites, predators, and those diabolic house snatchers, house sparrows and starlings. This means you need either a strategy for raising yourself to their height or, more practically, a pulley and winch system for lowering the house or gourds rack. After a nest check, be sure to reorient the house or gourd rack to exactly the same compass direction.

- Offer lots of housing—the Purple Martin Conservation Association recommends at least twenty-four units (not twenty-four houses), although they say twelve are enough to start with.

- Paint the house or gourds white. Trim can be any color.

- Open your housing at the right time. For unestablished sites, wait about four weeks after the first martins are expected to return to the area. But don't wait until martins actually come around—they recognize nesting sites by seeing open entrance holes, so leave a few open. Still, it's never too late to put up a martin house—even as late as September young birds may discover the site and return the following year to breed.

- Don't die until you've taught someone else how to manage your martin colony.

- For more about purple martins, see the notes with the gourd martin houses project.

CHICKADEE
WINTER ROOST

CLAUDIA OSBY

*"Even though I've lived on a farm most of my life, I never knew birds looked for a place to roost
in cold weather. I figured if they have enough sense to get in out of the cold,
the least we can do is give them some good, insulated shelter."*

CLAUDIA OSBY, ARTIST

WINTER ROOST BOXES

EVER WONDER WHERE BIRDS GO ON COLD NIGHTS IN NORTHERN CLIMATES? MANY ROOST IN TREE OR ROCK CAVITIES, DENSE UNDERBRUSH, OR EVERGREENS. SOME take shelter in nest boxes or, where they can find them, roost boxes like the projects here. The species that use roost boxes include bluebirds, tufted titmice, black-capped and Carolina chickadees, nuthatches, and some of the woodpecker family. In some cases, this protection means the difference between surviving the night and perishing from the cold.

Place roosts eight to ten feet off the ground on a tree or building, where they receive lots of sun and little wind. They should not be so large they can't hold body heat, and placing the entrance hole near the bottom also helps keep body heat from escaping.

The perches inside need to be staggered, so the birds aren't on top of each other. To make it easier for birds to grip and roost, roughen the perches with coarse sandpaper and consider tacking a piece of screen-door screen to the inside back. Plan the entrance-hole size and space the perches based on the size of the birds you hope to shelter (refer to nest box notes for each species).

The three roosts here all began with the same basic design, the chickadee winter roost.

A special feature of this roost is its extra layer of foam insulation, which can be added to any roost design. Here the outside of the roost allows you plenty of scope for creativity—stain it, paint it, decorate it, or simply enjoy the wood's natural beauty. (Other birds besides chickadees can use the roost, of course.)

TOOLS

Handsaw
Jigsaw or coping saw
3/8" drill
Drill bits (1/16", 3/8")
Screwdriver
Finishing hammer
Tape measure

MATERIALS

Red cedar or redwood, 3/4" thick:
   Front: 11-1/4 x 21"
   Backboard: 11-1/4 x 33"
   Roof: 11-1/4 x 13-1/4"
   Sides: 9-1/2 x 23" (2)
   Floor: 9-3/4 x 13"
3/8 x 36" dowel

SUPPLIES

2" finish nails
2-1/2" butt hinges (2)
3/4" foam insulation board scrap
Exterior wood glue
Paneling adhesive

BUILDING THE ROOST

■ **STEP ONE** Cut the backboard, sides, and floor. Then cut the roof and front to include a bevel on the rear edge of the roof piece and the upper edge of the front piece that matches the angle of the roof pitch.

■ **STEP TWO** Use the illustration to lay out the 2-1/2 x 3-3/4" entrance hole on the front and the 2-1/2 x 3-1/2" platform at the front of the floor. Cut with a jigsaw.

■ **STEP THREE** Mark the sockets for the three roost rods on one of the side pieces. Measured from the front and bottom edges, they are located at junctures of 2-1/2" and 9-3/4"; 5" and 13"; 7" and 16". Align the marked piece over the other side piece and drill 3/8" holes through both pieces.

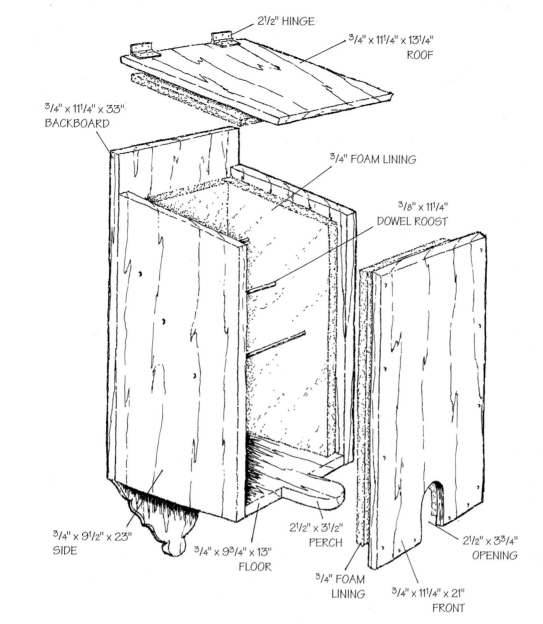

2½" HINGE

¾" x 11¼" x 13¼"
ROOF

¾" x 11¼" x 33"
BACKBOARD

¾" FOAM LINING

⅜" x 11¼"
DOWEL ROOST

¾" x 9½" x 23"
SIDE

¾" x 9¾" x 13"
FLOOR

2½" x 3½"
PERCH

¾" FOAM
LINING

¾" x 11¼" x 21"
FRONT

2½" x 3¾"
OPENING

■ **Step Four** Use the illustration to lay out the scalloped pattern on the lower part of the backboard. Cut with a jigsaw.

■ **Step Five** Set the edges of the two sides on the backboard, 2" below its upper edge. Fasten from the back, using glue and 2" finish nails spaced about 5" apart. Glue and nail the front, spacing the nails about 4-3/4" apart.

■ **Step Six** Fit the floor into the box and fasten it from the sides with 2" finish nails. Tilt the platform slightly toward the front to allow for drainage.

■ **Step Seven** Cut scraps of 3/4" foam insulation board to line the sides, front, and back, cutting it 3/4" back from the upper edges and removing a section for the entrance. Glue to the wood with paneling adhesive.

■ **Step Eight** Cut the 3/8" dowel into three 11-1/4" lengths. Tap these rods into the side holes and apply a dab of wood glue to the final 3/4" at both ends of each before aligning them with the sides of the box.

■ **Step Nine** Position the roof with the beveled edge against the backboard. Place the two hinges at the corners and mark the holes. Drill, and fasten with the hardware provided. Cut a piece of 3/4" insulation board to 9-1/2 x 9-3/4" and glue it to the bottom of the roof so it fits against the edges of the insulation already in place.

■ **Step Ten** Drill a hole near the top and bottom of the backboard for mounting. For siting tips, see "Winter Roost Boxes," page 86.

Note: Cedar and redwood are naturally weather-resistant and require no finish.

Bark Winter Roost

Nona Donaho

Spending a frosty night in a roost like this one should feel much like roosting in a tree cavity, only a lot more comfortable—for one thing, each bird has its own perch.

Tools

Jig saw
3/8" drill
Screw bit/countersink (no. 6)
Drill bit (1/16")
Hammer
Phillips screwdriver
Tape measure

Materials

Pine bark and twigs, moss
Cedar or redwood, 3/4" thick:
  Roof: 9-1/4 x 10"
  Floor: 9-1/4 x 11-1/2"
  Front: 9-1/4 x 22"
  Back: 9-1/4 x 30"
  Sides: 7-1/2 x 23-3/4" (2)
1/2 x 24" hardwood dowel

Supplies

1-1/2" decking screws (no. 6)
1-1/4" brads (16 gauge)
7/8" brads (18 gauge)
1" butt hinges (2)
Exterior wood glue
Acrylic exterior paint (brown)
Acrylic sealer (clear)

Building the Roost

■ **Step One** Follow the diagram to cut the roof, front, back, and two sides. One 9-1/4" edge of the roof should be cut with a bevel (slant) of about 15°. The front needs a 2-1/4 x 3" entrance hole. Cut the bottom piece as shown, with a 2-1/2 x 3-1/2" rounded platform extending from the floor.

■ **Step Two** Mark the locations as indicated on the two side pieces for the three inside dowel perches.

■ **Step Three** Drill the holes in the front, back, and bottom pieces using a screw bit. Assemble the box so the lower edges of the sides are 3-1/2" from the back's bottom edge. Use decking screws to join the front, back, and bottom to the sides.

■ **Step Four** Cut the dowel into three 7-3/4" lengths. Reach inside through the open top to place them at their marked locations. Secure them from the outside with 1-1/4" brads or screws.

■ **Step Five** Place the roof in position with the beveled edge toward the back. Fasten the two butt hinges with the screws provided.

■ **Step Six** Lightly paint the sides, the aprons at the top and bottom, and all sawn edges with the brown acrylic.

■ **Step Seven** Collect sturdy twigs about 1/2" in diameter: three 10" long, two 3-1/2" long, and one 20" long. Drill 1/16" holes through them and use 1-1/4" brads to fasten the 10" ones to the edges of the roof, the 3-1/2" ones to each side of the perch, and the 20" one just below the floor perch. Glue a handful of moss to the top surface of the platform.

■ **Step Eight** Collect pieces of fallen pine bark or bark from fallen trees and use glue and 7/8" brads to fasten it to the front and top surfaces.

■ **Step Nine** Spray the entire box with several coats of clear acrylic sealer. For siting tips, see "Winter Roost Boxes," page 86.

"I have a large pine tree whose bark falls off every year, so I used that and straight twigs off a wild dogwood we have to prune drastically every year. I suspect eventually I'll have to recover the sides of the roost with new bark. My hope is that the Carolina wrens around my house will use it—at least when it snows."

Nona Donoho, designer

BARN WOOD WINTER ROOST

ROLF HOLMQUIST

Feel free to adapt features from one roost to another—here you might consider adding a piece of wire screen to the inside back wall to give birds a "stairway" and a piece of foam insulation board under the roof for extra insulation.

TOOLS

Handsaw
Jigsaw
3/8" drill
Drill bits (1/16", 1/4", 3/8")
Screw bit/countersink (no. 8)
Hammer
Clamps
Tin snips
Phillips screwdriver
Tape measure

MATERIALS

Barn wood (or other found wood) of any thickness:
Front: 9-1/2 x 22"
Roof: 9-1/2 x 10"
Back: 9-1/2 x 30"
Sides: 8 x 24" (2)
Floor: 8 x 11"
3/8 x 30" hardwood dowel

SUPPLIES

2-1/4" decking screws (no. 8)
3/4" wood screws (no. 8)
6 x 9" old tin roof section
1" butt hinges (2)
Exterior wood glue

BUILDING THE ROOST

■ **STEP ONE**   Follow the diagram to cut the front, back, roof, and two sides. Cut a 2-1/2 x 3" entrance hole at the lower edge of the front piece.

■ **STEP TWO**   Cut the floor piece as shown, with a 2-1/2 x 3-1/2" rounded platform extending from the front. The width may have to be changed slightly to accommodate your wood's thickness.

■ **STEP THREE**   Mark the locations as indicated on one of the side pieces for the three inside dowel perches: 3", 6", and 9" down from the angled edge, and spaced evenly apart. Clamp the two sides together and drill 3/8" holes through both pieces at the marked points.

■ **STEP FOUR**   Place the shorter edge of one side piece against the front and drill four pilot holes with a number 8 screw bit, 5" apart. Glue and fasten with decking screws. Repeat the procedure with the other side piece.

■ **STEP FIVE**   Cut the 3/8" dowel into three 9-1/2" lengths. Tap them through the 3/8" holes in the sides of the box and glue the ends in place, with the dowels centered.

■ **STEP SIX**   Place the floor in position, recessed about 1/2" up from the box's lower edge. Trim the edges of the extended platform if necessary to make it fit. Drill two pilot holes through each side of the box and into the edges of the floor, and fasten it with glue and decking screws.

■ **STEP SEVEN**   Position the assembled unit onto the back, 1" up from the bottom edge. Use the number 8 screw bit to drill four holes about 5" apart into the sides. Fasten with glue and decking screws. Drill 1/4" holes near the top and bottom edges of the back for mounting.

■ **STEP EIGHT**   Center the roof tightly against the back piece. Fasten the two butt hinges by predrilling with the small bit and using the screws provided. Drill and fasten the small tin roof section at the top of the box and over the platform with short wood screws.

"This weathered barn wood I use has lots of cracks. To help weatherproof the roost and keep out drafts, I use carpenter's glue to seal up the cracks—just keep putting it in. Sometimes I use putty."

ROLF HOLMQUIST, WOOD ARTIST

BLACK-CAPPED, CAROLINA, AND MOUNTAIN CHICKADEES

area in its gray wing. (This is nothing; wait until you try identifying gulls.)

■

More clues: the black-capped's range covers Canada, Alaska, and the northern and western half of the United States; the Carolina's range lies south of the Great Lakes and west to mid-Texas; and the mountain's range runs from southwest Canada through the western states to Baja California.

■

Favorite habitats for black-cappeds and Carolinas are woods, willow thickets, parks, groves, and shade trees; mountain chickadees like mountain forests and conifers. These chickadees line their nest cavities with moss, grass, feathers, plant down, and hair or fur. All lay an average of six white eggs, the black-capped's and Carolina's marked with reddish browns. If disturbed on the nest, females of all three species hiss at intruders.

■

Everyone I know who has a bird feeder loves chickadees. Year-round residents, they hang off suet feeders all winter and hang around birdbaths all summer, their rasping "chick-a-dee-dee-dee-dee" as familiar as a robin's trill. Since chickadee flocks are territorial, each defending about twenty acres, you will have the same flock at your feeder from the end of one breeding season (August) to the start of the next, in early spring—the dominant pairs of the flock will then breed in the winter territory. The three U.S. species that sometimes use nest boxes are the black-capped, Carolina, and mountain chickadees.

■

The black-capped chickadee male feeds the female while she's incubating the eggs—slightly less than two weeks; fledglings fly after another two or three weeks.

■

Carolina chickadee pairs remain together all year, foraging in winter with small flocks that often include titmice, warblers, woodpeckers, and nuthatches.

■

Telling these three small, plump members of the titmouse family apart is the kind of exercise that makes other people ask birders "Who cares?" They graduate in size from the Carolina (4-1/2") to the black-capped (4-3/4-5-3/4") and the mountain variety (5-5-3/4"). All have the familiar black cap and bib, white cheeks, gray back, and buffy sides. *But,* the mountain chickadee has a white line above the eye, and the black-capped has a noticeable white

Mountain chickadees incubate their eggs for two weeks, then feed their young by regurgitation for the first four days. They too form forage flocks with other species in winter, often with sparrows, vireos, warblers, and bushtits.

Natural
Titmouse House

ROLF HOLMQUIST

Set on or near wooded land, a natural-looking house like this one appeals not only to tufted and plain titmice but to Carolina and black-capped chickadees, nuthatches, and downy woodpeckers.

Note: Because other birds and mammals that can't excavate their own cavities often depend on natural woodpecker holes, it's best to supply artificial houses for woodpeckers only in areas where no dead trees still stand, and only near a good source of insects such as water or fallen logs and ground debris.

TOOLS

Hammer or mallet
Wood chisel
Drill and 1/4" bit
Saw
Axe (optional)

MATERIALS

Chunk of hardwood tree trunk or branch, about 6 x 13-16" (minimum diameter, 6")
Barn wood, 1-1/2" thick:
   Roof: 6-1/2 x 12" *(or exterior plywood 1 x 8 x 8")*
   Bottom: 5 x 6" *(or exterior plywood 1 x 6 x 6")*
Branch cut in half for bottom front edge
Wood shavings (for woodpeckers)

SUPPLIES

2-1/4" galvanized flathead screws (9)
1/4 x 2-1/2" lag screws and washers for mounting (2)
Eye hook
Wood glue
Found items for ornaments

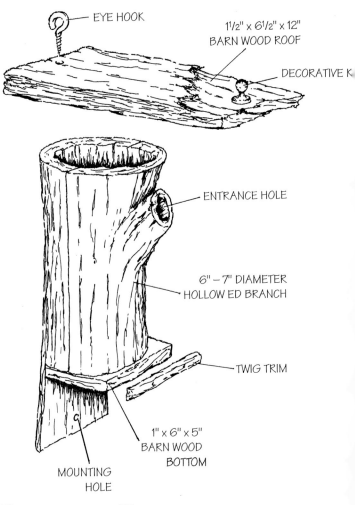

EYE HOOK

1¹/2" x 6¹/2" x 12"
BARN WOOD ROOF

DECORATIVE K

ENTRANCE HOLE

6" – 7" DIAMETER
HOLLOW ED BRANCH

TWIG TRIM

1" x 6" x 5"
BARN WOOD
BOTTOM

MOUNTING
HOLE

BUILDING THE HOUSE

Note: Predrill all holes to prevent splitting.

■ **STEP ONE**   Saw the top of the wood chunk at an angle for a sloped roof.

■ **STEP TWO**   Split the wood chunk in half lengthwise with a saw or axe. Cut the front half to about 9" in length.

■ **STEP THREE**   Cut and split the back so that the top section of about 9" matches the front, and the remaining bottom section is about an inch thick.

■ **STEP FOUR**   With a hammer or mallet and chisel, hollow out the center to form a hollow tube 4" in diameter the length of the wood when the front and back are fitted together.

"A word of warning. It's a lot more difficult to split and hollow out a piece of trunk with a knothole already in it. I'd recommend starting off with a plain log, free of any big branches or knotholes."
ROLF HOLMQUIST, DESIGNER

DOWNY WOODPECKERS

■

Downy and hairy woodpeckers are the despair of beginning birders. Both have dark backs with a white stripe down the middle, clear white underparts, and (males only) a red spot on the back of the head. Both range the length and breadth of the United States and southern Canada and enjoy similar habitats—orchards, river groves, woodlands, shade trees; sometimes they share the same tree. The downy is smaller (6-1/2"), but unless you happen to see one of each species side-by-side on a tree trunk, size is hard to judge. The distinguishing mark is bill length, easier to spot than you might think—hairy woodpeckers have noticeably long bills; downeys have almost ordinary-length bills. (Good luck!)

■

Downy woodpeckers go through elaborate courtship and territorial displays, both to attract mates and to repel invaders—they drum their feet, dance, wave their bills, and raise their crests. In courtship, male and female duet. Males seem to do most of the egg sitting, and fledglings are dependent on parents for food for up to three weeks.

■

As downeys are winter residents throughout their breeding area, they often use nest holes or boxes for shelter as well as for nesting and may also use winter roost boxes. They are frequent feeder visitors, especially if you provide suet.

■ **STEP FIVE** Drill an entrance hole 1-1/4" about 6-8" above the bottom of the front piece. Drill holes for two lag screws in the base (bottom of the back) and for the eye hook near the top of the back, for mounting. Cut at least two 5/8" ventilation notches anywhere near the top of the chunk.

■ **STEP SIX** Glue and screw the front and back together, using wood glue and four flathead screws. Glue and screw on the roof flush with the back in the same way, using three screws. Attach the floor with two screws only (no glue), so you can remove it for cleaning.

■ **STEP SEVEN** Glue a branch cut in half to cover the front edge of the floor. Attach found items as you wish (here, a brass doorknob and thick brass washers). Screw in the eye hook and the lag screws and washers for mounting.

PLAIN AND TUFTED TITMICE

Any small (5-6") crested, gray-backed bird in the United States is a titmouse. Tufted titmice range throughout the eastern United States to west Texas; plain titmice (whose crests are not tufted—a fine distinction) breed only in the western states, from Oregon and Idaho south, and prefer pinon-juniper and oak woodland. Both varieties have light rust flanks. Tufted titmice prefer woodlands, canyons, and shade trees or groves in towns.

■

Titmice nearly always keep the same mates from year to year, until one of the pair disappears. The female selects the nest site and stays glued to the nest until her five to nine eggs hatch; the male feeds her from courtship through hatching. In the warmer states, where tufted titmice usually have two broods per season, the young of the first brood sometimes help at the nest with the second brood. Plain titmice drive their young from the breeding territory as soon as they are self-sufficient.

Outside the breeding season, tufted titmice often flock with chickadees and, like them, are acrobatic food gatherers, clinging to twigs and perches upside down and sideways. Especially fond of sunflower seeds, they visit feeders all year long and scold intruders loudly (from a distance). Their clear whistle is often translated as "peter, peter, peter" or "peer, peer, peer."

HOUSE LOCATION AND TIPS

For downy woodpeckers, it's very important that you pack the house tightly to the top with wood shavings, so that they can excavate their own cavity. Face titmouse entrance holes away from prevailing winds, because titmice overwinter in northern states and sometimes use their nest boxes as well as artificial winter roosts for shelter. Ideal height: for titmice, from six to ten feet; for downy woodpeckers and chickadees, five to fifteen feet.

Note: If you intend this house for chickadees, make the entrance hole diameter one and one-eighth inches, put an inch of sawdust in the bottom of the box, and site it among hardwoods where it can get about 50 percent sunlight.

NUTHATCH HOUSE

CAROL BOMER

Besides nuthatches, this winged nest box should suit chickadees and house wrens. Hinging one of the "wings" would allow easy cleaning.

TOOLS

Jigsaw
3/8" drill
Drill bits (3/16", 1/4", 5/16")
1" spade bit or hole saw
Tack hammer
Straightedge
Scissors

MATERIALS

Redwood or red cedar, 3/8" thick:
Top: 2 x 6-1/2"
Roof: 4-3/4 x 8-1/2" (2)
Sides: 3-1/4 x 4" (2)
Front and back: 4 x 8-1/2" (2)
Bottom: 3-1/4 x 3-1/4"

SUPPLIES

4 x 18" sheet copper (12 gauge)
5/8" brads (18 gauge)
3/8" copper cut tacks
4" copper wire (12 gauge)
Wood glue
Green patina
Acrylic paint (ultramarine, white, and aqua pearl)

Note: If you intend this house for wrens or chickadees, make the entrance hole 1-1/8" across—house sparrows can move into any house with an entry whose diameter is at least 1-1/4". No directions are given for the perch, as perches (however charming) are not recommended for most houses.

BUILDING THE HOUSE

■ **STEP ONE** Use the diagram as a guide to cut and drill all the pieces.

■ **STEP TWO** Glue and position the sides between the front and back pieces, with the lower edges flush. Fasten the front and back with one 5/8" brad in each corner.

■ **STEP THREE** Slip the bottom piece in place, recessed 1" from the lower edges of the box. (Trim the edges if the fit is too snug.) Tap a 5/8" brad through each of the four walls to secure it.

■ **STEP FOUR** Cut a triangle from the copper sheet according to the dimensions in the diagram. Center it over the entry hole so its top point is 3/4" from the roof peak. Mark the outline of the hole from the rear, then cut the hole in the copper. Tack the copper triangle to the front with 3/8" tacks.

■ **STEP FIVE** Glue and tack the top piece to the roof peak with its front edge overhanging by 1-3/4". Then cut a 4 x 10" section of copper and form it over and around the wooden top. Fold the long edges under first, then tuck the lower corners up from underneath and fold the short edges over them and under, as you would wrap a gift. Use copper tacks at the corners and along the sides to secure the sheet.

■ **STEP SIX** Cut the two roof pieces into wing shapes, as shown in the diagram. Then use a bead of glue along each rear edge to fasten the slopes to the back of the house, with two 5/8" brads per side. The backs (shorter edges) of the wings should be flush with the back of the house. While the glue is still tacky, bend the roof pieces outward slightly at the front so the forward corners meet the edges of the top piece.

■ **STEP SEVEN** Cut two copper hinge-feathers according to the drawing. Bend and fasten them between the top and each of the roof slopes, using six copper tacks per side. Loop the 4" piece of copper wire through the holes as a hanger.

■ **STEP EIGHT** Brush a base coat of ultramarine blue on the wooden surfaces of the house. When it's dry, wash the white along the feathers, and follow with highlight streaks of aqua pearl. Once the paint has dried, add the green patina to the copper.

NEST BOX LOCATION AND TIPS

Nuthatches are less common users of nest boxes than some other cavity nesters, and you'll increase the likelihood of having them as box residents if you can locate the box in a mature stand of trees. The entrance hole needs to be one and one-quarter inches across, which also allows house sparrows into the box, a consideration if they live in your area. Place the box twelve to twenty feet above ground.

"I had so much fun working on this house, seeing it develop, not knowing exactly what I was going to do next. Anyone who makes it could use wing shapes or hand shapes—the whole theme is covering, protection. That's why we make birdhouses, isn't it?"

CAROL BOMER, ARTIST

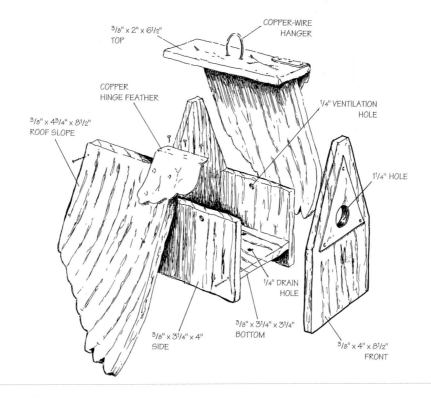

COPPER-WIRE
HANGER

3/8" x 2" x 6 1/2"
TOP

COPPER
HINGE FEATHER

3/8" x 4 3/4" x 8 1/2"
ROOF SLOPE

1/4" VENTILATION
HOLE

1 1/4" HOLE

1/4" DRAIN
HOLE

3/8" x 3 1/4" x 4"
SIDE

3/8" x 3 1/4" x 3 1/4"
BOTTOM

3/8" x 4" x 8 1/2"
FRONT

WHITE-BREASTED AND RED-BREASTED NUTHATCHES

If you spot a bird moving headfirst down a tree trunk, it's a nuthatch. The larger (5-6"), white-breasted variety lives year-round throughout most of the northern hemisphere; red-breasted nuthatches (4-1/2"), whose breasts are more pinkish-beige than red, prefer conifers and so nest mainly in cool, mostly northern climates, although they spread into the South in winter.

■

Although they prefer insects (which is why they're searching the bark), both these nuthatches visit feeders in winter for sunflower seeds and suet. Like titmice and chickadees, with whom they sometimes forage for food, nuthatches often open seeds or nuts by wedging them in a crevice of bark and hacking at them with their bills. (*Nuthatch* is from the Old French for *nut* and *ax*.)

■

Courting males bring food to females and bow or sway and sing to them, feathers fluffed. They build nests in natural wood cavities, deserted woodpecker holes, and in nest boxes like this one, where they make beds of shredded bark and other soft materials. Clutches of at least five eggs are common, white or pinkish white and marked with reddish brown. Eggs hatch in about fifteen days, and about three weeks later, the young are able to leave the nest. Pairs of white-breasted nuthatches guard the same feeding territory throughout the year, and a red-breasted pair may remain together through the cold months if enough food is available.

■

White-breasted nuthatches prefer deciduous forest land, woodlands, and forest edges. Red-breasted nuthatches nest mostly in conifers and in aspen woodlands. Both like mature stands with large decaying trees.

GOURD HOUSES FOR WRENS

HAROLD HALL

*"Using these basic directions, you can let your imagination dictate just how your gourd house will look.
I find my grass along the country roadside, but other materials, like straw, dried yucca leaves,
or dried leaves from trees in your yard will be just as effective."*

HAROLD HALL, DESIGNER, AMERICAN GOURD SOCIETY PRESIDENT

Bewick's, Carolina, and house wrens are more likely than any other birds to move into almost any house you make—or into an old shoe, clothes drying on the line, or hanging house plants. The creator of these gourd wren houses calls them "storybook birdhouses."

TOOLS

Drill (optional)
Sharp utility knife
Wood-burning tool
Sandpaper

MATERIALS

1 bottle gourd per house—for wrens, at least 5" in diameter and 6-8" deep
Small gourd or gourd pieces
Native grasses (for tall house)

SUPPLIES

Pot scrubber or steel wool pad
Sandpaper
1 lb. copper sulfate (for preserving)
Pencil
Waterproof glue
Clear acrylic finish or varnish
Stain (for roofs, detail, and green house)
Wire

MAKING THE HOUSE

Note: Although Hal Hall has designed his gourd houses with perches, they are not included in the instructions, as perches attract house sparrows.

- **STEP ONE** Soak the gourd in soapy water and scrub it clean, then let it dry.
- **STEP TWO** Drill or carve an entrance hole (1" diameter for house wrens only, 1-1/8" for both kinds of wren and chickadees) high enough up so the bird can step down into the house. Shake the seeds out through the opening, then file the sides of the entrance smooth with sandpaper wrapped around a pencil.
- **STEP THREE** Drill or carve three small holes in the bottom of the gourd for drainage.
- **STEP FOUR** Drill a hole through the top of the gourd to thread a wire through for hanging. (You can quit here for a simple gourd house. As far as the birds are concerned, it's ready for occupancy.)
- **STEP FIVE** To ensure years of use, preserve the gourd by following the directions in "Tips for Gourd Birdhouses," page 105.
- **STEP SIX** To decorate your gourd with windows, doors, or other designs, draw the design on with a pencil. Wood burn over the lines and erase any pencil marks that still show.
- **STEP SEVEN** Carve canopies for doors or windows from pieces of another gourd and glue them on with waterproof glue, trimming and sanding as needed to fit.
- **STEP EIGHT** For each gourd shown here, see the additional directions with the individual photograph.

GOURD LOCATION AND TIPS

Hang wren gourds in early April in the South, early May in the North. House wrens nest five to ten feet off the ground, under the eave of a building or in a tree. A gourd hung near a brush pile or dense underbrush should prove almost irresistible to Carolina wrens, who may also use it as a winter roost. All wrens seem to appreciate a home that gets a little sun. Houses for wrens are among the only houses that can hang free from an eye screw or tree branch; most birdhouses should be firmly anchored. When a wren family vacates the gourd, clean it out as best you can to ready it for another brood. (Break up the nest with the handle of a wooden spoon, then shake and pull the pieces out.)

the next clutch. Each male has a repertoire of from twenty-seven to forty-one different song types (songs that vary in how the syllables and phrases are put together); paired males and females sing duets.

BEWICK'S WRENS

■

Like all wrens, Bewick's characteristically cock their tails up (rather than down, like bluebirds), have longish, slightly downcurving bills, and are small—Bewick's are 5-1/4"—and gray-brown with light breasts. With practice, you can distinguish Bewick's from other wrens by their longer tail with white edges and white eyebrow stripe (but Carolina wrens have a white eye stripe too).

■

Frequent birdhouse dwellers and once common from southern Canada to Mexico, they are now declining east of the Mississippi. They breed in open woodland, shrubland, farms, and suburbs and, as insect eaters, spend most of their time in thickets, underbrush, and gardens.

HOUSE WRENS

■

If you can get close enough or use binoculars, you can distinguish this small (4-1/2–5"), lively, gray-brown, light-breasted bird from other wrens by the light-colored ring around its eye.

■

In courtship the male, tail raised and wings aquiver, sings to the female, after which they often go together to inspect the nest he has under way. Male house wrens are quite fierce about their breeding territory and the security of their homes. To confuse predators, they often build dummy nests, stuffing sticks and other material into many nest boxes and cavities in the area of their real nest. Both male and female often destroy the eggs of other birds nearby, including those of other house wrens.

■

House wrens breed throughout North America except in the southern states, southern California, and southwestern Arizona, where they spend the winter. They usually have two broods of six to eight eggs each, which hatch in thirteen days; the young fly about twelve to eighteen days later.

△ CAROLINA WRENS

■

Large for a wren at 5-3/4", Carolinas are beloved by beginning birders for their distinctive, usually three-syllabled, very loud song: "tea-kettle, tea-kettle, tea-kettle." They have cinnamon backs, buff underparts, and conspicuous white eyebrow stripes.

■

Resident throughout the eastern United States to mid-Texas, these wrens frequent thickets and brush piles, suburban gardens, and towns; they'll visit suet and sunflower seed feeders in winter. The Carolina wren population has been on the decline in the Northeast and parts of the Midwest; providing protected nesting sites will help slow this loss.

■

Carolina wrens make long-term, committed neighbors. Pairs remain together on a permanent territory throughout the year; unlike many songbirds, they don't fly south for the winter. The male prepares the nest and feeds the young—usually five—while the female begins

TIPS FOR GOURD BIRDHOUSES

THE FIRST BIRDHOUSE IN NORTH AMERICA MAY WELL HAVE BEEN A GOURD—WE KNOW AT LEAST THAT EARLY NATIVE AMERICANS HUNG THEM FROM TREE BRANCHES. *Today, depending on gourd size, where they are hung, and the size of their entrance holes, these houses may attract Carolina, Bewick's, and house wrens; chickadees; purple martins; and violet-green and tree swallows. (See project directions and notes on each species for construction and siting details.) The gourd artists represented in this book each have developed their own techniques for creating bird abodes from gourds.*

Placing entry holes correctly can mean the difference between hosting birds and killing them. If you drill or carve the hole too high, rain will come in and drown the newly hatched birds. If you drill too low, the nestlings can fall out. Always cut the entry hole exactly perpendicular to the vertical axis of the gourd when it is suspended—that is, along the outermost part of the curve, pointing neither upward nor downward.

Preserve your gourd after cleaning it out by submerging it in a solution of one pound copper sulfate to five gallons of warm water. Completely submerge the gourd for about fifteen minutes—you can hold it under with a brick (wear rubber gloves). Drain and let dry for several days before painting. (This solution is toxic to the environment and may be saved for years; don't flush it into a septic tank.)

Caution: Gourd dust can burn your skin. Always wear a tight-fitting dust mask while drilling and cleaning out gourds and when removing nests from them.

Paint this storybook gourd house with clear acrylic or varnish. For the grass roof, make bundles of six or seven pieces of grass, glue them together, and set them aside to dry. Glue the bundles around the gourd in overlapping layers, working toward the top. Hide the stubble ends of the top row by gluing on a cap from another gourd, then trim the grass around windows, doors, and roof line, and elsewhere as needed.

▲

For the shingled roof of this gourd wren house, cut half-inch rectangles from pieces of other gourds, varying the size to create a random look. Beginning at the widest part of the gourd, near the entrance hole, glue the shingles around the gourd, overlapping each new row and using smaller shingles near the top. Staggering the line looks more natural. Glue on a roof cap from the top of another gourd to hide the top of the final row of shingles. When the glue is dry, stain the shingles and the house in contrasting colors, then waterproof with several coats of clear acrylic finish or varnish.

▶

The line for the roof on this gourd wren house is wood burned, then the roof is stained with cherry stain. Paint the whole house with varnish or clear acrylic finish.

SUNFLOWER
NESTING SHELF

STEVE MITCHELL

Although perfect for nesting American robins, this sunny shelf also works fine for tree swallows and eastern phoebes.

TOOLS

Circular saw or handsaw
Coping saw
3/8" drill
Screw bit/countersink (no. 6)
1/4" drill bit
Phillips screwdriver
Tape measure

MATERIALS

Western red cedar, 11/16" thick:
    Back: 9-1/8 x 13"
    Roof: 7 x 8"
    Floor: 8 x 8-5/8"
    Sides: 6 x 8" (2)

SUPPLIES

1-1/2" decking screws (no. 6)
Small can or juice glass

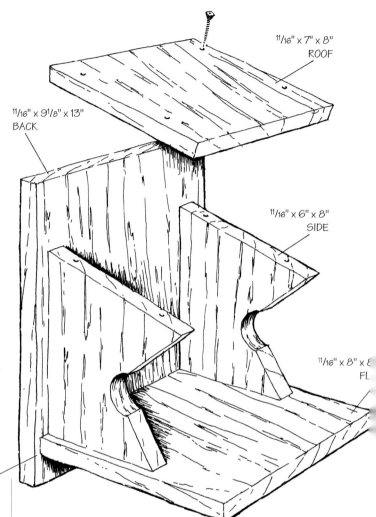

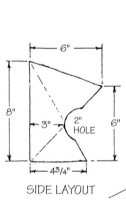

SIDE LAYOUT

BUILDING THE SHELF

■ **STEP ONE** Cut out the back, roof, floor, and sides using the photo as a guide. Place the roof piece in place against one of the completed side pieces and mark the angle at which the bevel must be cut to meet the back. Cut that bevel into the roof.

■ **STEP TWO** Use a small can or a juice glass to scribe a 1"-radius half-circle at the V-juncture on each side piece. Use a coping saw to remove the wood at those marked points.

■ **STEP THREE** Position the roof on the top edges of each side piece so the back and the sides are flush. Drill four mounting holes and fasten with decking screws.

■ **STEP FOUR** Center the assembly on the back piece so the roof is 2" from the top edge. Mark, and drill four mounting holes through the back and into the side pieces. Fasten with decking screws.

■ **STEP FIVE** Center the bottom against the lower edges of the sides. Drill through the bottom and fasten with four decking screws.

■ **STEP SIX** Drill 1/4" holes through the back near the top and bottom edges and mount the shelf.

SHELF LOCATION AND TIPS

If you especially want to attract robins, try siting your nesting shelf under an eave, soffit, or other sheltering house feature or above a light fixture. You can also put it on a tree—however, if cats or raccoons or other predators are a threat, add a predator guard of some kind. Robins seem especially fond of birdbaths—George Harrison in *The Backyard Bird Watcher* reports counting nine young robins at once wading in his small pool.

"I wouldn't put this shelf more than five feet off the ground, because the fledgings can't really fly right away. Robin young are among the first to hatch. They kind of flutter down out of the nest and walk around awhile before they fly."

STEVE MITCHELL, WOODWORKER

AMERICAN ROBINS

■

Say "bird" and most of us in the United States would say "robin." No wonder, for robins touch down at some time of the year everywhere in North America, and the only places they don't breed are in parts of Florida and the Southwest. Along with barn swallows and most waterfowl, American robins migrate by day, probably navigating by the sun.

■

These familiar birds (9-11"), with brick-red breasts and gray backs, frequent suburban lawns, towns, farms, and forests. They find earthworms by sight, not sound, as many of us might have guessed.

■

Robins fiercely defend their cup-shaped mud nests, built on unkempt foundations of twigs and grass. They have two, occasionally three broods a year of from three to seven young. (You can spot young robins by their rusty speckled breasts.) The male takes care of the fledglings from the first brood while the female sits on the next set of eggs.

Robins build their nests on shelves and ledges of buildings and other structures, in bushes, sometimes on the ground, and almost anywhere they can get support—here, in a front-door wreath. (The human family used another door until the young robins left the nest.)

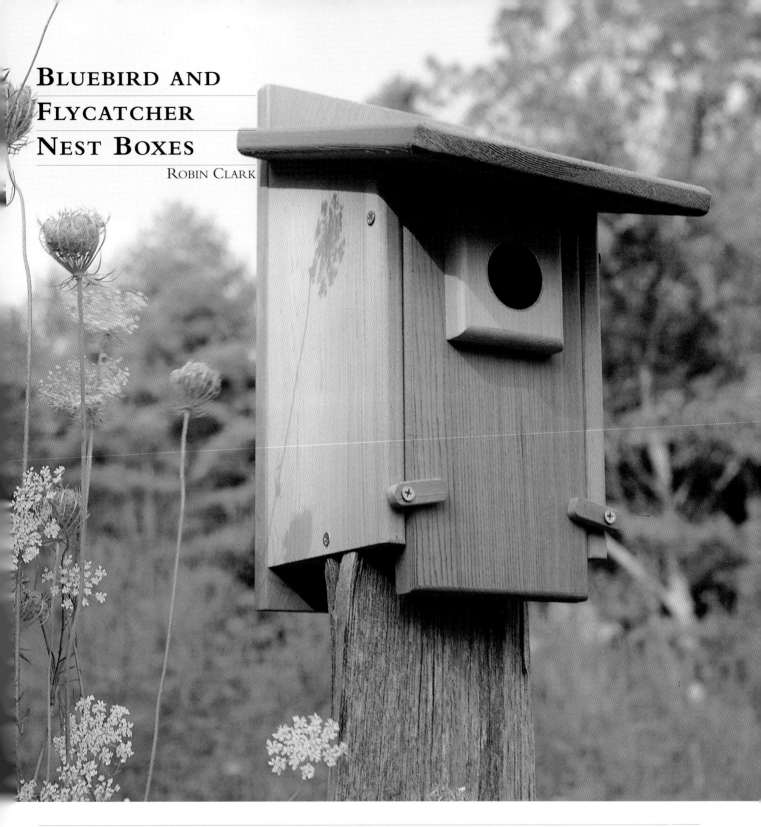

BLUEBIRD AND FLYCATCHER NEST BOXES

ROBIN CLARK

"I added the copper ring around the entry hole as an optional feature—
it's a good way to help prevent predators from gnawing into the box.

ROBIN CLARK, WOODWORKER

A versatile abode, this nest box will serve eastern, western, and mountain bluebirds, great crested flycatchers, and violet-green and tree swallows, depending on its site and entry hole size.

TOOLS

Circular or jig saw
Coping saw
3/8" drill
Drill bits (1/8", 1/4")
1-1/2" spade bit or hole saw
Screw bit/countersink (no. 6)
Phillips screwdriver
Protractor
Tape measure
Palm sander

MATERIALS

Western red cedar, 11/16" thick:
  Back: 6-3/8 x 13"
  Sides: 5-11/16 x 10" (2)
  Door (front): 5 x 8-1/4"
  Floor: 5 x 5"
  Roof: 8-3/4 x 9-3/8"
  Predator guard: 3 x 3"
  Latches: 5/16 x 1-1/2" (2)

SUPPLIES

1-1/2" decking screws (no. 6)
3/16" flat washers
1 x 1-1/2" rigid copper pipe (optional)

BUILDING THE NEST BOX

■ **STEP ONE** Use the diagram as a guide to cut and drill the door, back, sides, and predator guard. Do not bore the large entry hole yet. Cut the floor and trim off the corners as shown, and cut the roof with a 17° angle in one 8-1/4" edge. Round all edges with a palm sander and coarse paper.

■ **STEP TWO** Cut the two toggles with a coping saw so that the wood's 11/16" thickness becomes the face. Each finished piece should be 5/16" thick and 1-1/2" long, with rounded ends. Drill the screw holes 3/8" from the end of each one.

■ **STEP THREE** Fasten the predator guard to the door, centered and with one edge 5-1/2" from the door's lower edge. Use two decking screws drilled and driven from the back face. Drill a 1-1/2" hole for blue-

birds and swallows (1-3/4" for great crested flycatchers), centered and 7" from the door's lower edge, through the guard and the door behind it.

■ **STEP FOUR** Fasten the sides to the back, leaving a 1" overhang at the lower edge. Attach the bottom to the back and sides.

■ **STEP FIVE** Fasten the door to the sides, flush with the forward edges, and with a space at the top and a 1" overhang at the lower edge. Leave the screws slightly loose so the door can pivot.

■ **STEP SIX** Fasten the roof to the sides with the angled edge against the back.

■ **STEP SEVEN** Drill the latch mounting holes in the front edge of each side piece, 1" from the lower edge. Fasten with decking screws and two flat washers behind each latch. Slip the copper pipe section into the predator guard opening.

Note: If raccoons live in your area, reinforce the latches with large-headed pivot nails to keep birds more secure.

BOX LOCATION AND TIPS

For great crested flycatchers, place the nest box in an orchard, along the edges of woodlands, or in woodlands, ideally from ten to twenty feet up. (For bluebirds, see directions and tips on page 114.) These birds often have to battle starlings for nesting sites.

MOUNTAIN BLUEBIRDS

∎

Like a bright speck of summer sky, the male mountain bluebird is turquoise blue all over; the female is grayish brown with touches of blue on tail, wings, and rump. About seven inches (the size of a large sparrow), they eat mainly insects, adding fruit to their diet in winter.

∎

These birds breed in most of the western and southwestern states and in western Canada, often at elevations of 7,000 feet and higher. Once the female has chosen the site, the pair constructs a loose cup-shaped nest of grass, pine needles, and twigs. They produce pale blue to whitish eggs, usually five or six in each of two batches, and brood them for about two weeks. The young fly in twenty-two or twenty-three days.

∎

Mountain bluebirds raised in nest boxes imprint on them, or "bond" to them, and as adults will choose the same kind of box for nesting.

GREAT CRESTED FLYCATCHERS

∎

A warm-weather, mainly eastern U.S. resident of groves and woodlands, the great crested flycatcher is a cardinal-sized bird (8-9"). You're less likely to see one than to hear one whistling high in a tree, making a loud "wheep, wheep." Should you spot one, you will know it by its bright yellow belly, gray breast, and orange red to cinnamon wings and tail—it may or may not push up its bushy crest.

∎

These insect-eating birds build bulky nests of leaves, adding in such materials as fur, feathers, and sometimes snake skin. They raise one brood a year, averaging broods of five. Eggs are creamy white or beige, marked with lavender, olive, and browns; the young hatch in about two weeks and fledge in about three. Keep an eye out for them—small balls of feathers clinging to tree trunks.

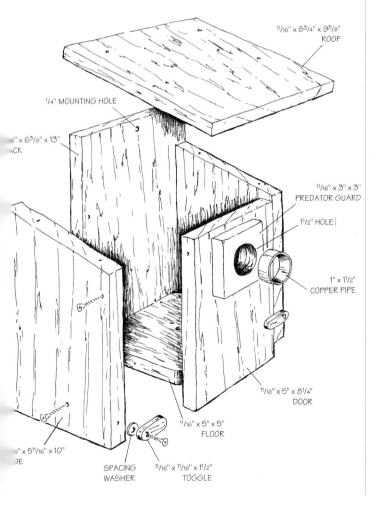

Peterson Bluebird Nest Box

Claudia Osby

This designer version of the Peterson bluebird house—a model many feel is the ideal bluebird nest box—is both eye-pleasing and easy to check and clean out.

Tools

Table saw
Jigsaw or coping saw
1-1/2" hole saw
3/8" drill
Drill bits (1/16", 1/4", 1/2")
Finishing hammer
Nail set
Tape measure
Protractor
Paint brush

Materials

Pine, 3/4" thick except where noted:
   Front: 4-1/2 x 14-1/2"
   Inner roof: 4-1/2 x 8-3/4"
   Backboard: 4-1/2 x 29-1/4"
   Floor: 4-1/2 x 4"
   Face strip: 4-1/2 x 5/8"
   Outer roof: 9-1/4 x 12-1/2"
   Sides: 9-1/2 x 16-1/2" (2)
   Spacers: 3/8 x 3/8 x 4" (2)
   *   3/8 x 3/8 x 3-1/2" (2)*

Supplies

1-1/2" finish nails
3/4" brads (18 gauge)
1/4 x 4 x 4-1/2" hardware cloth
Exterior wood glue
White water-based stain
Light-blue acrylic paint
Polyurethane varnish

Building the House

- **Step One** Cut the floor, inner and outer roof, face strip, and spacers to the sizes indicated.

- **Step Two** Cut the front, sides, and backboard to the rough sizes indicated. Use the illustrations provided to draw the scallops on those pieces, then cut them with a jigsaw.

- **Step Three** Drill a 1/2" hole 2" from the top and rear edge on both side pieces. Drill a 1-1/2" hole 1-3/4" from the top of the front piece. Starting 3" from the top edge, cut eighteen saw grooves 1/8" deep and 3/8" apart on the inside face of the front piece.

- **Step Four** Cut a 65° angle on the upper edge of the backboard and complementary angles into the front and rear edges of the roof so they're parallel to the backboard's length. Cut 65° angles into one 4-1/2" edge on the floor and inner roof.

- **Step Five** Sand the outer face of all pieces and apply a water-based stain/acrylic blue wash coat. Leave the inner faces unfinished.

- **Step Six** Fasten the four spacers to the upper face of the floor with 3/4" brads, flush to the edges. Toe nail the inner roof and floor to the backboard 1/2" and 11", respectively, from the inside edge of the backboard. (*Toe nailing* is hammering in the nails obliquely, or at a diagonal.)

- **Step Seven** Fasten the sides to the edges of the backboard with glue and finish nails spaced 3-1/2" apart. Raise the upper corners of the sides 3/8" above the upper edge of the backboard.

- **Step Eight** Secure the inner roof and floor from the sides with 1-1/2" finish nails. Nail the face strip to the front edge of the inner roof.

- **Step Nine** Position the front with its upper edge 3/8" from the bottom of the face strip and flush with its face. Drive a 1-1/2" pivot nail into each side 3/4" from the front's upper edge. Drill a 1/16" hole through the side near the bottom edge and lightly tap in a finish nail to keep the front secure. This nail can be removed with pliers for cleaning.

- **Step Ten** Fasten the roof to the sides with glue and three finish nails spaced 4" apart along each side. The rear edge should be flush with the backboard.

- **Step Eleven** Drill two 1/4" holes through the backboard for mounting. Place the hardware cloth on top of the floor spacers.

"I used the blue wash in honor of the bluebirds, of course. We're moving out to the country this year and we'll finally be able to put up some bluebird boxes. I grew up on a farm, and I can't wait."

CLAUDIA OSBY, ARTIST

EASTERN AND WESTERN BLUEBIRDS

■

The Rockies mark the division between eastern and western bluebirds, although small numbers of each species wander across the border and the two have much in common. Males have a hunched look when perched, mostly blue backs, and rusty red breasts; the main distinction is the western's blue throat. Females are paler, duller in color. Both species are slightly larger than sparrows, the eastern at seven inches, the western a bit smaller.

■

Courting male bluebirds sing and flutter in front of females, then perch beside them, preen their feathers, and sometimes offer food. Bluebirds produce pale blue (sometimes white) eggs and brood them for about two weeks. They usually have two broods a season of four to six young each; the young of easterns make their first flight in fifteen to twenty days (field data on westerns are less reliable).

■

In winter, eastern bluebirds gather in flocks of a hundred or more and often roost in nest boxes, alone or in small groups. If you leave a box open to shelter them in cold weather, watch out for four-footed interlopers—deer mice and white-footed mice.

BOX LOCATION AND TIPS

All three U.S. bluebird species prefer nest boxes in open, sunny locations on fence posts or other posts, five to six feet up, about 100 yards apart. (Bluebird houses on trees expose the birds to predators—raccoons and cats.) Although they will sometimes nest in rural backyards or in the outer suburbs, the ideal site for bluebirds combines grassland and scattered trees or posts—golf courses, farms, cemeteries, prairies, and so on.

Nest boxes need to be in place by late February in the South, late March in the North. The entrance hole should face east, northeast, or north to keep the sun from overheating the box. Plan on checking the house every few weeks to remove nests of birds you don't want in it. If you have left a nest box up through the winter, be sure to check it early to clear out any mice who might have wintered there—they may destroy arriving birds. Once a bluebird brood has left the house, clean it out so that the pair can produce a second brood there.

Since house sparrows and mice also like bluebird nest boxes, the farther you can put the house from buildings, the more chance you give the bluebirds. If you find tree swallows competing with bluebirds for these nest boxes, try putting two of them about 25 feet apart—one for the bluebirds, one for the swallows. Because of bluebirds' territoriality, nest boxes for bluebird pairs need to be at least 100 yards apart.

In this century, bluebird populations dropped seriously with the advent of DDT (now banned), the decline of available natural nesting sites (dead trees, branches, fence posts), and more competition from other species, especially house sparrows and starlings. (Eastern bluebirds declined by 90 percent; nest boxes like this one have been maintaining their numbers at that level for several decades.) Bluebirds defend their nests fiercely and frequently drive off invading tree swallows, house sparrows, and house wrens; still, many people choose to help them by destroying the nests of other bird species (often removing house sparrows and starlings altogether) and by cleaning out the piles of twigs left by wrens.

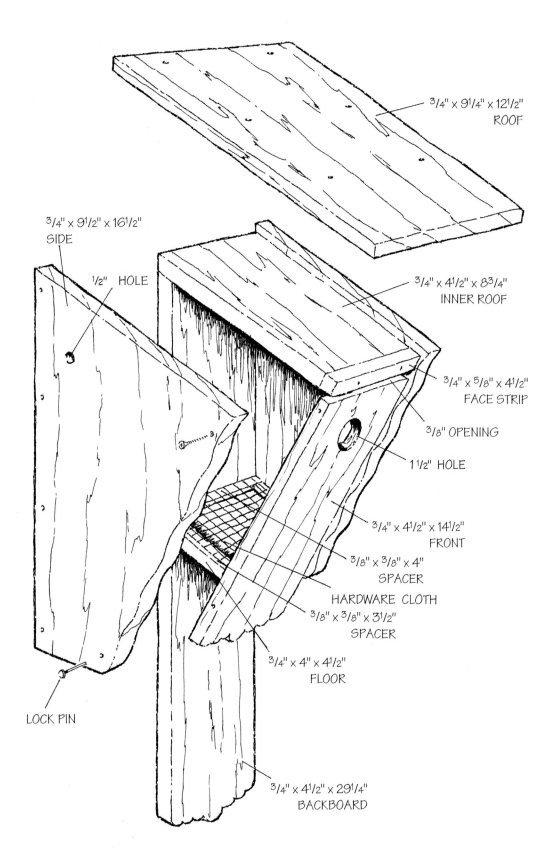

3/4" x 9¹/4" x 12¹/2"
ROOF

3/4" x 9¹/2" x 16¹/2"
SIDE

¹/2" HOLE

3/4" x 4¹/2" x 8³/4"
INNER ROOF

3/4" x 5/8" x 4¹/2"
FACE STRIP

3/8" OPENING

1 ¹/2" HOLE

3/4" x 4¹/2" x 14¹/2"
FRONT

3/8" x 3/8" x 4"
SPACER

HARDWARE CLOTH

3/8" x 3/8" x 3¹/2"
SPACER

3/4" x 4" x 4¹/2"
FLOOR

LOCK PIN

3/4" x 4¹/2" x 29¹/4"
BACKBOARD

RANDOMWEAVE
BIRDBATH

CARLA FILIPPELLI

Not all birdbaths have to be concrete or plastic. Hang this randomweave bath basket near a patio or on an apartment balcony to offer your bird guests a delightful and unusual place to cool off on a summer day.

TOOLS AND MATERIALS

Garden clippers
Tape measure
1 lb. of 5 mm round rattan reed (no. 7)
1 lb. of 3/4" flat rattan reed
Shallow 9" terra cotta, glass, or plastic dish
Clear polyurethane spray

WEAVING THE BATH

■ **STEP ONE**   Using the round reed, make a coiled handle 17 x 11"—coil the reed three times, each time weaving it in and out of itself and laying each coil on top of the one before. (If you haven't worked with round reed before, you'll find that its lengthwise grooves fit together when pieces of reed are laid on top of or next to each other.)

■ **STEP TWO**   In the same way, make a 10" coil of round reed and attach it perpendicular to and inside the handle where you want the basin/basket to be, about two-thirds of the way down. This coil forms the rim of the basin/basket body.

■ **STEP THREE**   With more round reed, form a basket shape large enough to hold a shallow 9" dish. Loop the reed through the rim on one side, up, and down through the rim on the opposite side. Continue interweaving this way until you have formed the general shape you want.

■ **STEP FOUR**   With flat reed, fill in the random spaces and shape the basket, weaving over, under, around, and through. Be sure to keep the flat reed smooth as you weave, laying it in along the plane of the shape you've framed in.

■ **STEP FIVE**   Finish the weaving with round reed, filling in the remaining open spaces. Attach it to the rim every so often for stability, and weave it occasionally through the base of the handle. If you choose to, at this point you can also wrap the handle of the basket a few more times with round reed to make it thicker.

■ **STEP SIX**   Weatherproof the finished birdbath by spraying it with polyurethane, if you wish.

"Randomweave is more creative and conceptual than lots of weaving— there are few rules and no traditional patterns, no certain number of spokes. The artist determines when it's done, how open to make it. It's truly a right-brain technique."

CARLA FILIPPELLI, BASKET MAKER

VINE BIRD FEEDER

PAULA HEDRICK

Nuthatches, chickadees, titmice, and cardinals—along with squirrels and chipmunks—seem to find this two-decker feeder irresistible. Just the other morning a Carolina wren perched on the upper hoop and sang a brief ode to winter.

TOOLS AND MATERIALS

Garden clippers
Awl
2 lengths of sturdy, woody vine for hoop handle
Bendable vines (Virginia creeper, honeysuckle)
Round reed (no. 6)
Wire

WEAVING THE FEEDER

■ **STEP ONE** For the main frame, or hoop, bend one large, woody vine into a circle and wire the ends together. For the handle, bend the remaining large vine into a U-shape that will fit the diameter of the first circle.

■ **STEP TWO** Decide how much curve you want in the back of the feeder (the bottom of the basket), and then cut eleven pieces of number 6 round reed to that length for the spokes that will run from one edge of the main frame to the other.

■ **STEP THREE** Wrap one flexible vine twice around one end of the hoop, catching the start of the vine as you wrap. Holding the first spoke on the inside center of the hoop's rim, bring the vine under the rim to the right of the spoke. Make an X with the vine by crossing it over the spoke, over the rim to the left of the spoke, around and under the rim there, then back over the rim and the front of the spoke to the right. Wrap the rim twice, then repeat the X-lashing with a second and third spoke, one on each side of the central spoke. After the last two turns around the rim, weave over and under all spokes and the rim until the weaving vine

runs out. Repeat this process to lash the other ends of the three central spokes to the other side of the frame.

■ **STEP FOUR** Continue weaving in this manner, adding spokes as gaps open. It's important always to add one spoke to each side to maintain an odd number of spokes. Weave for about 4", then stop weaving around the rim of the hoop. (This will leave the gaps in the sides of the feeder.) Weave around the last spoke on each side instead. Alternate the weaving on both sides of the feeder until you nearly reach the center, where you will attach the platform.

■ **STEP FIVE** To make the frame for the feeding platform, first use the awl to make a hole in the center of each spoke. Cut a piece of number 6 reed to the diameter of the inside rim of the hoop plus 1/2". Make a hole in the side of the hoop on each side deep enough to insert this crossbar reed into. If the ends won't stay in the hole, use a dab of hold-anything glue. Now use the awl to make holes in the crossbar reed opposite the holes in the spokes.

■ **STEP SIX** Measure the distance from the back of the feeder (the bottom of the basket) to the crossbar. Cut eleven pieces of reed about 1/2" longer than that measurement. Insert one end of each piece of reed into a spoke hole and the other end into the corresponding hole in the crossbar. (You can glue these, too, if you need to.) Cut off any excess reed.

■ **STEP SEVEN** To fill in the platform, weave over one, under one with a flexible vine. If you wish, wrap the crossbar with a vine to hide the round reed.

■ **STEP EIGHT** Finish weaving the main part of the feeder with vines.

■ **STEP NINE** Turn the feeder on end, then lash the ends of the U-shaped handle to the sides of the basket with wire, as in the photo. Then wrap the lashings with vines, making an X.

"If you use materials from the woods or garden, this project costs nothing to make. Just go out and look for stuff that will bend—if it bends you can weave with it. If the weaving on the platform doesn't turn out tight enough to hold seed, you can cover the platform with sheet moss."

PAULA HEDRICK, BASKET MAKER

SALT BOX AND SAUCERS BIRD FEEDER

NELS ARNOLD

Plenty of adults like to mess around with clay as much as kids do. This feeder makes a good joint venture—or everyone can make their own.

Note: This clay requires firing in a kiln—often these are accessible through local public schools, community colleges, or community art classes.

WHAT YOU NEED

Utility knife or other sharp knife
About 4 lbs. of earthenware clay (fires cone 06-04)
Ruler
Rolling pin
Plastic wrap
Tape
Salt box or similar cylinder
2 saucers, salad plates, or other forms for top and bottom
3 leather strips or shoe laces, 26-30" each
Metal hanging ring (optional)

WHAT TO DO

■ **STEP ONE** Cover your working surface with cloth. With the rolling pin, roll out the clay into a rectangle about 3/8-1/2" thick.

■ **STEP TWO** Measure the height of your salt box and the distance around it. On the clay, draw a rectangle whose sides match these two measurements. Lay a straight edge along each side to cut out the clay rectangle with the knife.

■ **STEP THREE** Cover the salt box with plastic wrap and tape it. Put the box on the clay rectangle and roll the clay up around it. Pinch all along the sides where the edges meet to seal them. Smooth the edges out. If you want to, roll the clay-covered salt box on an onion sack or some other interesting surface to make designs.

■ **STEP FOUR** Stand the clay-covered box up and let it dry until you can take the box out and the clay will stand up by itself.

■ **STEP FIVE** Turn the two saucers upside down. Cover the bottoms with plastic wrap and tape them.

Make one ball of clay about as big as a tennis ball for each saucer. With the rolling pin, roll each ball out into a circle, like a pizza, about 3/8-1/2" thick.

■ **STEP SIX** Cover the bottom of each saucer with a clay circle. Trim the edges with the knife. Let them dry until they can hold their shape without the saucer.

■ **STEP SEVEN** You need all three forms stiff enough to hold their shape, but not dry. Smooth the inside edges of the cylinder. At the bottom of the cylinder, cut three small openings, like little tunnels, where birds can get the birdseed. These should be about the same distance apart from each other, around the cylinder.

■ **STEP EIGHT** Set the cylinder on the smaller clay saucer you made. Draw around the bottom with a knife. Lift the cylinder back off. Scratch its bottom and the circle you drew on the saucer, so they will stick together better. Smear some very wet, gooey, soft clay (called *slip*) on the bottom of the cylinder and on the circle. Stick them together.

■ **STEP NINE** Put the big clay saucer on top of the cylinder. Make three holes around the rim of the saucer big enough for one shoelace or leather strip to go through, to hang the feeder up. They should be the same distance apart from each other. Now make three holes in the rim of the bottom saucer right under the top three holes. The shoelaces or leather strips will go through both saucers and fasten underneath the bottom saucer.

■ **STEP TEN** Take the top saucer off. Now is the time to decorate the feeder however you want to. You could press shapes into it, carve designs, or add clay leaves or acorns. Do whatever you like. Then let all the pieces dry for about four or five days. Don't try to dry them too fast, or the clay may crack. When the pieces are dry, they need to be fired in a kiln to cone 06-04 (this means heated in a special oven to a certain temperature).

■ **STEP ELEVEN** Knot the shoelaces or leather together under the bottom saucer, or knot each lace under one hole. Then feed them through the holes in both saucers so they join about 12" above the top saucer. This way you can raise the lid of the feeder to fill it. Either knot them together at the top or attach them all to a metal ring for hanging.

"There's practically no limit to the ways you can decorate this feeder. Make it textured by impressing objects into the clay, like a pine cone, peach seed, shell, tree bark. Or you can carve designs, or attach clay leaves, flowers, or birds with clay slip."

NELS ARNOLD, POTTER

ABODES FOR OTHER BACKYARD BEASTS

WHETHER WE LIVE IN AN APARTMENT WITH A FIRE ESCAPE BALCONY, IN THE COUNTRY, OR IN THE SUBURBS, SOME FORM OF WILDLIFE LIVES NEARBY. THIS MEANS that if we want to, we can entice some of them to dwell near enough to get better acquainted with. The behavior of common creatures like gray squirrels, mice, turtles, bees, flying squirrels, and toads can be fascinating to watch, close up or (for some of us) from a distance.

Making safe homes or resting places for such creatures brings us rewards we probably don't even suspect when we begin planning and shopping, sawing and fitting and painting.

PREENING AND SUNNING RAFT

MARK STROM

"This is a project people should really be able to play with. For instance, if you use green willow logs and get the raft in the water before they dry out, they'll sprout and give the ducks some shade. I recommend putting a branch underwater for the turtles and ducks to climb up on."

MARK STROM, WOOD SCULPTOR

If you are fortunate enough to live beside a lake or to have a pond of any size on your property, you probably host ducks and turtles sometime during the year. Among the species that would welcome a safe haven like this raft for rest and relaxation are mallards, wood ducks, blue-winged teal, and painted turtles.

TOOLS

Handsaw
Hammer
Tape measure
Rasp
3/8" drill
1/8" drill bit

MATERIALS

Willow or cedar logs:
  Floats: 4" diameter x 26" (3)
  Decking: 2-1/2" diameter x 60" (7)

SUPPLIES

4" 20-penny galvanized nails (2 lbs.)
1/4 x 1" galvanized bolts with nuts (4)
8" hollow-core concrete blocks (2)
2 lengths 3/16" welded coil chain

PAINTED TURTLES

■

Painted turtles (4–10"), named for the bright red borders on their shells and yellow markings on their black heads, are the turtles most likely to be found in any small pond in the northern U.S. or southern Canada. They eat crayfish, insects, and mollusks and hibernate in mud underwater.

BUILDING THE RAFT

■ **STEP ONE**   Choose your wood from sources such as fence posts, deadfall, or cut saplings. Trim all pieces to length and round the ends with the wood rasp.

■ **STEP TWO**   Predrill 1/8" holes in the decking pieces if necessary to prevent splitting. Position the three 26" float pieces 17" apart, measured edge-to-edge. Center the first 60" decking piece over the floats, 3" in from one end and with approximately 7" of overhang at each side. Fasten the decking to the floats using two galvanized nails at each joint.

■ **STEP THREE**   Place and fasten the remaining six decking pieces to the floats in the same manner, spacing each piece no more than 1/2" from its neighbor. The finished platform will measure 26 x 60".

■ **STEP FOUR**   Loop one end of each chain section through the space and around the floats at opposite corners of the platform and secure each end to a link of its chain using a 1/4 x 1" bolt. The opposite ends should be looped through the core holes of the concrete block and fastened in the same manner.

RAFT LOCATION AND TIPS

To anchor the platform, set the blocks about eight feet apart in three feet or so of sunny, sheltered water just offshore and out of reach of predators. The chain should be long enough to allow a foot or so of slack at high water. To be certain the raft won't sink once it becomes waterlogged, you can fit sheets of rigid polystyrene plastic underneath.

MALLARDS, BLUE-WINGED TEAL, AND WOOD DUCKS

■

These three ducks are marsh species and belong to the dabbler family of ducks—that is, rather than diving for their food, they feed on the water surface by dabbling and upending themselves. All dabblers can take flight vertically. Like most ducks, these three species perform a fascinating variety of courtship displays—head and tail shaking, wing flapping, bill tossing, neck stretching and arching, and so on.

■

Mallards (20-28") range throughout North America, as do the smaller blue-winged teal (15-16"), except in the central eastern states. Teals favor fresh ponds and marshes, while the less choosy mallards frequent almost any body of fresh water—marshes, rivers, lakes, swamps, and ponds. The dramatically marked wood ducks (17–20-1/2") occur mostly in rivers, ponds, and wooded swamps in the eastern United States and in the Northwest, including northern California.

YOU CAN CONVERT A RAFT INTO A PLATFORM FOR A CANADA GOOSE NEST WITH A WASHTUB, METAL CUTTERS, METAL PUNCH, NAILS, AND SAWDUST. USE A ROUND metal washtub twenty-two inches across, ten and a half inches high. Punch about ten holes in the bottom for drainage. Cut an escape route for the new goslings right under the upper edge of the tub, six inches wide and four inches high.

Paint the washtub a natural color, then nail it in the center of the raft. Fill it a third full of sawdust, with an armload of grass or wild hay on top. In the northern United States, you should have platforms in place by mid-March (on the ice or in water), later in warmer climates, about twenty to thirty feet from shore in two to four feet of water.

About Canada geese. If you're lucky, some fall or spring you'll see a long V-shaped wedge of migrating Canada geese, honking their way through the October or March sky. The most abundant North American species, these black-headed geese with their distinctive white chin strap breed in the northern states west of the Mississippi, in the western states except California, and along the Atlantic coast.

Canada geese nest from early April through mid-May, producing one brood a year of four to seven goslings; eggs hatch in about four weeks. When an intruder threatens its nest or young, the male goose tries to distract it by feigning injury. The male also is the parent who usually leads the goslings to water. These birds form long-term pairs, although their average life span in the wild is just a few years.

Tudor Flying Squirrel and Mouse House

CLAUDIA OSBY

White-footed and deer mice often move into nest boxes meant for bluebirds, chickadees, wrens, nuthatches, and prothonotary warblers, all of whom can also nest happily in this house.

Tools

Table saw
Jigsaw or coping saw
1-1/4" hole saw
3/8" drill
Drill bits (1/16", 1/4")
Screw bit/countersink (no. 8)
Phillips screwdriver
Finishing hammer
Nail set
Tape measure
Protractor

Materials

Pine, 3/4" thick except where noted:
Floor: 4 x 3-3/4"
Sides: 4 x 8-7/8" (2)
Front & back: 7 x 12" (2)
Roof: 6-1/8 x 7-7/8" (2)
Backboard: 5 x 23"
Roof scallops: 3/8 x 1-1/2 x 7-3/4" (2)

Supplies

1-1/2" finish nails
1-1/2" decking screws (no. 8)
Exterior wood glue
White water-based stain
Acrylic paint in desired colors (here—white, brown, gold, blue, pink, red)
Polyurethane varnish
Sandpaper
Paintbrushes
Brown grocery bag
#2 pencil
Tracing paper

Building the House

- **STEP ONE**   Cut the front, back, floor, roof, sides, and backboard pieces. Rip a length of 1 x 2" to make the 3/8" stock for the roof scallops.
- **STEP TWO**   Trim the 4" edges of the floor at an 81° angle and drill four 1/4" holes 1" from each corner. Cut one 6-1/8" edge of each roof piece to an 83° angle so the peak joint meets evenly. Duplicate this angle on the ends of the two scallop pieces. Trim one 4" edge of each side piece at a 48° angle and drill two 1/4" holes 2-1/2" apart 1-1/4" below the upper edge.
- **STEP THREE**   For mice, wrens, and chickadees, drill a 1-1/8"-diameter entry hole in the front piece centered 8-1/2" from the bottom edge. (For flying squirrels or nuthatches, the entry hole should be 1-1/4" in diameter.)   Cut seven saw grooves 3/8" apart into the inner face of the front piece, just below the hole. Use a table saw blade to make these no more than 3/8" deep.
- **STEP FOUR**   Use a jigsaw and the illustrations provided to cut the scallops on the roof trim and the backboard.
- **STEP FIVE**   Sand all pieces well and stain the outside, then sand again with a piece of brown grocery bag.
- **STEP SIX**   Paint the pieces as you wish. To paint a house like the one shown here, trace the pattern onto a piece of tracing paper. Then rub the lead of a #2 pencil across the back of the paper over each line. To transfer the pattern to the wood, lay the pattern on the wood, pencil-rubbing side down, and trace over the lines.
- **STEP SEVEN**   Using acrylic paints, to reproduce the house shown in the photo, first paint the front door brown. (You can make board marks with black paint

"This style of painting is much easier than it looks—no one should be afraid to try it. But if you don't want to paint the house decoratively, you can just paint it all one color or maybe paint the trim a second color."
CLAUDIA OSBY, DESIGNER

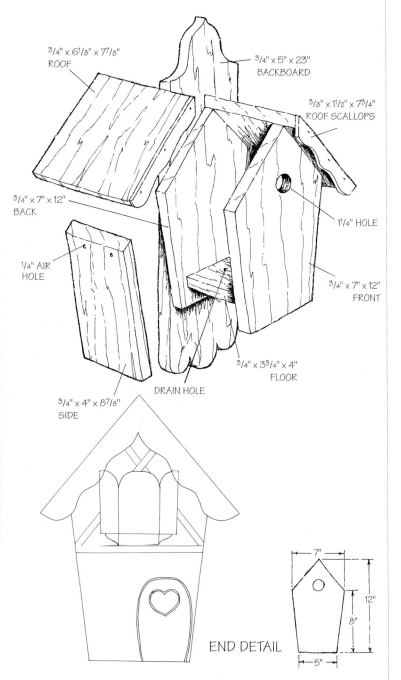

ROOF 3/4" x 6 1/8" x 7 7/8"

BACKBOARD 3/4" x 5" x 23"

ROOF SCALLOPS 3/8" x 1 1/2" x 7 3/4"

BACK 3/4" x 7" x 12"

1 1/4" HOLE

1/4" AIR HOLE

FRONT 3/4" x 7" x 12"

FLOOR 3/4" x 3 3/4" x 4"

DRAIN HOLE

SIDE 3/4" x 4" x 8 7/8"

END DETAIL

7"

12"

8"

5"

flower boxes. Dot in flowers with a heavy red paint (red is translucent)—you may have to go over them again after the first dots dry. Dab a few white dots around for a light and airy feeling. Freehand paint a vine on the side going over the door; add leaves and berries if you like. Along the bottom paint flowers, grass, or shrubs.

- **STEP EIGHT** Coat the outer surfaces with polyurethane varnish. Leave the inside unfinished.

- **STEP NINE** Fasten one side between the front and back pieces using glue and three 1-1/2" finish nails.

- **STEP TEN** Slip the other side into place and drive one pivot nail through the front and back exactly 1" down from the top front edge. These nails must be even. Drill a 1/16" hole 1" from the lower edge at the front and lightly tap in a finish nail. This can be removed with pliers to open the door for cleaning.

- **STEP ELEVEN** Position the roof pieces flush to the back with the peak forming a tight joint. Glue and fasten with eight 1-1/2" finish nails.

- **STEP TWELVE** Fasten the scallops to the front edge of the roof with six 1-1/2" finish nails.

- **STEP THIRTEEN** Position the house 5-1/4" up from the lower end of the backboard. Use a number 8 screw bit to drill two holes through the backboard and into the back. Fasten with decking screws.

HOUSE LOCATION AND TIPS

If mice move in during the winter and you want to convert the house for birds in the spring, clean out the mice and their nest by early March and check the box often to be sure they haven't moved back in. Cover the entry hole in winter if you prefer to keep mice out altogether.

Place mouse houses on fence posts about three or four feet above the ground with the entry hole facing east or southeast, away from cold winter winds. It's okay to open the door for an occasional peek at growing mouse families. *Caution: Avoid contact with mice or nests; these mice carry deer ticks, which are carriers of Lyme disease.*

The one-and-one-quarter-inch entrance hole for flying squirrels and nuthatches will also admit house sparrows; you can discourage sparrows by placing nest boxes meant for flying squirrels on trees in heavily wooded sites, the higher the better—they often choose cavities twenty to thirty feet up.

using the chisel end of a flat brush.) Paint the door handle and hinges gold, windows and shutters a medium blue gray. Make board marks with black on the shutters and diagonal white lines on the windows using the same method. Paint the boards on the gable ends brown. Paint the roof the same blue as the shutters. Thin brown paint with a little water to paint the flower boxes with a brown wash. Dab in greenery in the

NORTHERN AND SOUTHERN FLYING SQUIRRELS

■

Even hardened wildlife observers find flying squirrels charming. This is an animal, writes nature observer Ted Williams, "that stamps its feet when angry; lies on its back and kicks to discourage nest snoopers…greets members of the same denning group by literally kissing them."

■

If you have a bird feeder and mature hardwood trees near your house, you probably have flying squirrels. Any squirrel you see at night is either a flying squirrel or an insomniac squirrel of another species—flying squirrels are our only nocturnal variety. (Because they are quite tame, you can easily watch them by dimly illuminating your feeders at night.) They have huge dark eyes and are much smaller than gray squirrels, only about nine inches from nose to tail tip compared to about nineteen inches for grays. Their backs are reddish brown or grayish brown, their underparts white, and they are able to glide because of a loose flap of skin, the patagium, that extends from each foreleg wrist to each hind-leg ankle.

■

In woodlands and backyards throughout the eastern United States, there are more southern flying squirrels than any other squirrel. They traditionally live in abandoned woodpecker holes or natural tree cavities or build nests in attics and under roofs—clear-cutting and the clearing of dead trees has greatly reduced their numbers.

■

Flying squirrels usually breed in early spring and again in midsummer, the litters averaging three hairless young weighing in at half an ounce each, who make their first flights about five weeks later and are weaned at seven weeks. While they don't hibernate, during cold spells groups of flying squirrels curl up together in their nests for warmth.

WHITE-FOOTED MICE AND WOODLAND DEER MICE

■

These two species look and act so much alike there's no need to distinguish them here. The handsomest of the more than 250 U.S. species of the mouse family, deer mice and white-footed mice (five to nine inches, including tail) weigh less than an ounce and have light brown backs and white undersides and feet. Both have large ears and large, prominent black eyes. (They cannot be mistaken for the dull-gray city house mouse with its long scaly tail, a European import.) Like cats, they groom and clean themselves daily.

■

The breeding season in the North runs from February to November; each female can produce at least four litters a season, with an average of four babies per litter. The young stay clamped to the mother's nipples most of the time, a protective measure in case the mother must flee the nest. They are mature at six or seven weeks.

■

These mice are nocturnal, plentiful, and will eat almost anything. Besides woodpiles and burrows, they often move into cabins, cottages, hunting camps, and wooded suburban homes, although they rarely travel more than five hundred feet from their birthplace. Still, they usually survive less than a year in the wild—they are hunted by most meat-eating creatures.

SQUIRREL NEST BOX

MARK STROM

Squirrels make me think of such maxims as "One person's treasure is another's trash," or "Beauty lies in the eye of the beholder." Many people who feed birds spend a lot of time trying to discourage squirrels from setting foot on their property—a futile exercise, nearly all admit. This box is not for them, but for the many others of us who enjoy squirrels for their cleverness, bravado, and entertainment value.

TOOLS

Circular saw
Jigsaw
3/8" drill
1/4" drill bit
Screw bit/countersink (no. 8)
Phillips screwdriver
Hammer
Chisel
Square

MATERIALS

Red cedar, 3/4" thick:
    Back: 9-1/4 x 26"
    Roof: 9-1/4 x 12-1/4"
    Bottom: 9-1/4 x 6-3/4"
    Sides: 9-1/4 x 16-1/4" (2)
    Front: 9-1/4 x 18"
    Acorn: 4-1/2 x 7"

SUPPLIES

1-1/4" decking screws (no. 8)
1-1/2" finish nails
1" finish nails
1" butt hinges (2)
Exterior wood glue

BUILDING THE BOX

■ **STEP ONE** Cut out all pieces. Use the illustration to duplicate the acorn pattern on both ends of the back piece and one end of the roof. Cut out the shapes with a jigsaw. Drill a 1/4" mounting hole centered 1-1/2" from each end through the back piece.

■ **STEP TWO** On the back piece, mark a line across the face 4" down from the top. Draw lines angled at 45° to the right and left, spaced 3/4" apart in a cross-hatch pattern. Use a chisel to carefully cut straight down on each line, repeating the process until the line is cut to its full length. Then make angled cuts into the first cut, beginning about 1/16" to one side. Repeat until all the lines are completed.

■ **STEP THREE** Measure down 3-1/2" from the top of one side piece and mark a point in the center of the board. Use a cup or jar lid to draw a 3"-diameter circle around this point. Drill a 1/4" hole at the edge and cut the opening with a jigsaw. On the other side piece, drill four ventilation holes equally spaced about 3" down from the top.

■ **STEP FOUR** Position the two side pieces 1/2" in from the edges of the back and 4" down from the top. Fasten from the back using glue and 1-1/2" finish nails.

■ **STEP FIVE** Mount the front piece to the sides in the same manner, with all upper edges flush and the sides recessed by 1/2".

■ **STEP SIX** Slide the bottom into position flush with the bottom and side edges. Glue and fasten with 1-1/2" finish nails.

■ **STEP SEVEN** Drill two 1/4" ventilation holes through each side, 1-1/4" in from the upper corners.

■ **STEP EIGHT** Position the roof on top of the box and mount the butt hinges about 6" apart, using the hardware provided.

"I chose an acorn design for this box because of the squirrels, naturally, but you could put any kind of decoration or design you want on it. There's plenty of scope for the imagination on a big, plain box like this. You could do wood carving, or wood burning, or paint it—have a good time, that's the main thing."

MARK STROM, WOOD SCULPTOR

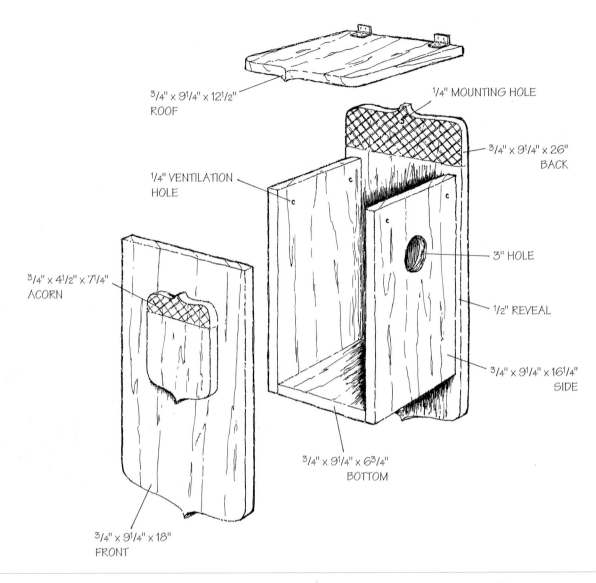

3/4" x 9 1/4" x 12 1/2"
ROOF

1/4" MOUNTING HOLE

1/4" VENTILATION
HOLE

3/4" x 9 1/4" x 26"
BACK

3/4" x 4 1/2" x 7 1/4"
ACORN

3" HOLE

1/2" REVEAL

3/4" x 9 1/4" x 16 1/4"
SIDE

3/4" x 9 1/4" x 6 3/4"
BOTTOM

3/4" x 9 1/4" x 18"
FRONT

■ **STEP NINE** Measure in 3" from the center of the front edge of the roof and drill a hole with a number 8 screw bit. Fasten the roof closed with a decking screw.

■ **STEP TEN** Cut the acorn shape from the 4-1/2 x 7" piece using a jigsaw. Draw a line down the center lengthwise, and one across, 2" below the top. Draw the cross-hatch pattern and cut with a chisel as before. Fasten the finished acorn emblem to the face of the box with glue and 1" finish nails; position it 2-1/2" below the upper edge.

Note: You can make the box even more attractive to squirrels if you give them a perch to stand on to look out: nail a 4" piece of 2 x 2" across the inside of the nest box 4" beneath the entrance hole.

BOX LOCATION AND TIPS

Fill your squirrel box half full of dry leaves and hang it in the fall on a tree at least ten inches in diameter, ideally twenty to thirty feet up. Attach it with a lag screw and washer at the top and bottom of the rear piece. You don't need to clean the box out, but don't forget to loosen the lag screws each year to allow for the tree's growth.

GRAY SQUIRRELS

■

The good news about gray squirrels is that they're everywhere—easy to identify, fun to study or just to watch. The bad news is that they're everywhere—hogging all the birdseed at feeders, littering the ground with sharp nut shells, shrieking at you as you sit on your own patio or try to enjoy a peaceful hour at a quiet campground or park.

■

The eastern gray squirrel ranges throughout the United States and southern Canada east of the Rockies and measures eight to eleven inches plus a bushy tail at least that long. (The slightly larger western gray lives west of the Rockies and is similar in behavior; the Arizona gray lives in Arizona, New Mexico, and Mexico. These notes apply to the eastern and western gray.)

■

Squirrels don't hibernate, although they can stay in their dens for up to two weeks during severe cold spells; in fact, male squirrels are communal and as many as thirteen have been known to den together. Gray squirrels also don't memorize all the places they bury nuts. They recover buried nuts by smell, even under a foot of snow, more often than not nuts cached by another squirrel. (They also eat fruits, seeds, flowers, mushrooms, birds' eggs, and, sometimes, nestlings.)

■

Squirrels usually chase each other for one of two reasons: to drive intruding squirrels out of the host territory or to mate. Gray squirrels can produce both a winter and a summer litter of three to five half-ounce babies. They are weaned and on their own at ten to twelve weeks.

FOX SQUIRRELS

■

Larger, rarer, and more reclusive than the gray squirrel, the fox squirrel looks different in different parts of the country—tawny brown all over in much of its range from the Great Plains east, but dark with white feet, nose, and ear tufts in the Appalachians, for example. It seems to have flourished mostly in the Midwest, where it lives in towns and cities as well as in its preferred open pine forests and deciduous woodlands.

■

We know less about these hermits of the squirrel world than about other species. They produce at least one litter a year (in February or March), weigh about two pounds, and are more likely than other squirrels to stay on the ground for longer periods when pursued. They resemble gray squirrels in their eating and food storing habits and are especially fond of corn.

RED (CHICKAREE OR DOUGLAS) SQUIRRELS

Smaller, noisier, and more excitable than gray or fox squirrels, red squirrels have been known to chew flimsy birdhouses to bits, perhaps for the flavor of the glue. In winter they are reddish with white bellies, in summer more olive-yellow. At about thirteen inches, including a five-inch tail, they weigh in at around seven ounces. Red squirrels occur throughout the United States and Canada wherever spruce, fir, and hemlock dominate.

■

They build nests of bark shreds, grasses, and leaves, usually in tree cavities or boxes but sometimes in the crotch of a limb or even in a burrow underground, often beneath a stone wall. Red squirrels store food in the ground, often building large caches of up to a bushel of fodder. Their varied diet includes nuts, seeds, berries, flowers, fungi, birds' eggs, and an occasional nestling. They wedge mushrooms in tree crevices to dry before eating or storing them.

■

Red squirrels have two breeding seasons (March-May and July-September) and often produce two broods of three to six young a year, weaning them in about six to eight weeks.

MASON BEE HOUSES

ROBIN CLARK

"The main requirement for bees is flowers. These bee houses can be mounted on a post or a tree trunk or set on a stump or rock in a garden or orchard—or near one."

ROBIN CLARK, WOODWORKER

MATERIALS

Western red cedar:
   Post: 3-1/2 x 3-1/2 x 8"
   Roof: 11/16 x 4 x 4-1/2"

SUPPLIES

1-1/2" decking screws (no. 6)
6" copper wire (12 gauge)

BUILDING THE HOUSE

■ **STEP ONE** Cut a slice off the top of the 8" post for the roof slant (a 17° slant in the photo).

■ **STEP TWO** Drill 5/16" holes one inch apart on the front of the house, evenly spaced in rows of three across and six down, and about 1-1/4" deep.

■ **STEP THREE** In the roof piece, drill two 1/8" pilot holes centered about 1-1/4" and 2-3/4" from the back edge. Bevel the back edge to fit the slant of the house. Screw the roof to the house with two decking screws.

■ **STEP FOUR** On the center back of the house about 1-3/4" below the roof, use the number 6 screw bit to drill a 1/8" pilot hole for hanging. Loop the copper wire in half around a screwdriver or pencil. Force the ends of the wire into the pilot hole, then bend the wire so the loop is above the roof. Fasten a screw in the pilot hole to secure the wire.

Although these abodes are called mason bee houses, several other kinds of solitary bees who tunnel into dead or soft wood may find them inviting, such as carpenters and leaf cutters. Not to mention cuckoo bees, mentally unequipped to build their own nests anyway. Still, like all bees, even cuckoo bees are a boon to gardeners and plants as pollinators of fruits and flowers. (Above, a variant.)

TOOLS

Handsaw
3/8" drill
5/16" drill bit
Screw bit/countersink (no. 6)
Tape measure
Phillips screwdriver

MASON BEES

■

Every mason bee is—essentially—queen for life. Unlike honeybees and bumblebees, which are social insects and live in colonies, mason bees belong to the class of solitary bees, which live alone. Nevertheless, as the bee house would indicate, they often nest close together. Each builds her own nest, stores her own pollen and nectar in the cells, lays an egg in each cell, then seals the nest and moves on.

■

These bees get their name from the variety of mason bee that attaches its nest of mixed clay and saliva to stones or walls—it looks as if someone has thrown a small ball of clay against the wall.

TOAD HOUSES

AUSTIN SCONYERS-SNOW
AND FRENCH SCONYERS-SNOW

Toads eat bugs, live just about anywhere, and never fight or get upset. If you have a piece of shady land with some bushes on it, plenty of insects, and some cool, damp dirt to hide in, you have the perfect place for a toad.

WHAT YOU NEED

Medium-sized clay flowerpot
Old clay flowerpot or pieces of pot
Acrylic paints, including white
Paintbrush
Trowel or large spoon

WHAT TO DO

■ **STEP ONE** Wash and dry the flowerpot if it has dirt on it. Wash and dry the old pot or pieces of pot.

■ **STEP TWO** Do some practice painting on the old pot or pot pieces, to see how the colors will look. To make light colors, try mixing white with each of the other colors. To get good, clear colors on your pot, paint on the white acrylic first and let it dry. Then paint another color on top of it.

■ **STEP THREE** Paint designs or flowers or whatever you think a toad would like on the outside of the pot you are using for your toad house. If you like the way the paint looks over white acrylic, paint the white on first. When it's dry, paint the colors over it. Let the paint dry.

■ **STEP FOUR** Find a good, shady hiding place outside. Under a bush is a good spot. Bury the pot on its side halfway in dirt. Make sure the dirt inside the pot is a little wet and crumbly. Put a few dead leaves and twigs inside too. You'll know when a toad moves in by the way the dirt at the front of the house gets worn down—that's where the toad sits and waits for its dinner to pass by.

"I tried out some different ideas, and the flowers turned out the best. We worked with only primary colors—you can make any color you want from them. Too bad we don't have any toads in our yard—Lucy, our dog, would eat them."
AUSTIN SCONYERS-SNOW, NATURALIST

"I love to draw, and I thought these colors would look pretty. I love toads. I've seen a toad in Florida at my aunt's house, sitting in the rain. I'm going to give her my toad house."

FRENCH SCONYERS-SNOW, ARTIST

AMERICAN TOADS

■

Here are some toad facts that not everyone knows. Toads aren't slimy, and touching one won't give you warts. A toad can't poison you. It never rains toads.

■

If you ever get close to a toad, you will see that it has shining golden eyes. Toads are usually brown, but some have many colors, with patches of yellow, orange, and red.

■

Toads and frogs look kind of alike. They both used to be tadpoles. They both lay their eggs in water. But frogs have smooth, wet skin and long legs. Toads have dry, warty skin and short legs. Frogs leap. Toads hop. Frogs like to stay near water. Toads live in backyards and gardens and on mountains, almost anywhere that is shady and has dirt.

■

In one summer, a toad can eat about 10,000 insects. It also eats beetles, spiders, snails, worms, frogs, and other toads. A toad tongue is sticky and fastens at the front instead of the back. It snaps out like a yo-yo, faster than we can see, sticks to a piece of food, and flips it back in.

■

Lots of things spit toads out instead of eating them because they shoot out a poison that causes itching (not for people). But the poison doesn't hurt snakes, skunks, crows, owls, hawks, or herons. They like the way toads taste. When a toad thinks it's about to get eaten, it blows up like a little balloon to look bigger and scarier.

GRAPEVINE SKEP

DON DANIELS

"Watch out—once you start experimenting with grapevine, you can get hooked.
It's inexpensive or free, and you'd be surprised what you can make out of it.
One of the things I've made is a headboard for a bed."

DON DANIELS, ARTIST

Designed as an ornament, this skep would add a graceful natural accent on a table or in an atrium, on a deck, apartment balcony, or porch.

TOOLS AND MATERIALS

Pliers
Side cutters or garden shears
Armload of grapevine
Tie wire

BEFORE YOU START

If your grapevines are dry, before step 5 separate out the vines you will use to wrap your skep, soak them in water, bend and tie them as shown, and let them dry in this horseshoe shape.

WEAVING THE SKEP

■ **STEP ONE**   Make two circles of grapevine 12" across, one circle 3" across, and one circle 1" across.
■ **STEP TWO**   For the base, cut four 14" pieces of vine for cross pieces. Wire the ends of the cross pieces to the rim of one circle and in the center as shown, as if you were making a spoked wheel.
■ **STEP THREE**   For the frame, cut four 36" pieces of vine for uprights. Wire the ends of two uprights evenly spaced around the base, forming two arches, as shown. Insert the other 12" circle inside the arch about two-thirds of the way up the uprights and wire it in place.
■ **STEP FOUR**   Wire the 3" circle of vine to the center top.
■ **STEP FIVE**   Wrap your frame with vines, and for a final touch, add the 1" circle as an "entrance," as shown.

RANDOMWEAVE SKEP

CARLA FILIPPELLI

Woven beehives—or skeps—have been around at least since the Middle Ages, when European farmers wove them of straw and kept honeybees in them. (*Skep* comes from the Old German word *skepfen*, to shape.) Today's skeps are purely for fun and decoration.

TOOLS AND MATERIALS

Garden shears
1/2 lb. of 1" flat rattan reed
1 lb. of 5 mm round rattan reed (no. 7) or grapevine, honeysuckle, or Virginia creeper

WEAVING THE SKEP

■ **STEP ONE**   Make a coil 14" across using the round reed. Wrap the coil three times, each time weaving it in and out of itself and laying each coil on top of the one before. (If you haven't worked with round reed before, you'll find that its lengthwise grooves fit together when pieces of reed are laid on top of or next to each other.)
■ **STEP TWO**   With another piece of round reed, form the overall shape of the skep, which is about 15" high, by looping the reed through the rim on one side, up, and down through the rim on the opposite side. Continue interweaving this way until you have formed the general shape you want.
■ **STEP THREE**   Weave the 1" flat rattan reed through the form, filling in the random spaces left by the round reed. Remember, you are forming the walls of the skep—be sure to keep the flat reed smooth as you weave.
■ **STEP FOUR**   Finish the skep by filling in the random spaces with as much round reed as you like. Tuck in or clip loose ends. Check to make sure the skep sits well and that the shape is well balanced and pleasing to you.

DESIGN NOTE

If you're a beginning weaver, allow three or four hours for this project.

"My original influence for the randomweave technique and style came from a species of weaver birds we saw in a Florida aviary. I also saw an anthropological study about nomads who built their structures every night from sticking poles in the ground and weaving in natural materials. We built a couple of these in our yard."

CARLA FILIPPELLI, BASKET MAKER

CONTRIBUTING ARTISTS

LEWIS APPLEBAUM
Brush Creek Gardens
180 Sigmon Road
Fletcher, NC 28732

NELS ARNOLD
30 Bishop Cove Road
Fairview, NC 28730

CAROL BOMER
Soleil de la Gloria
140 Avondale Ridge Road
Asheville, NC 28803

ROBIN CLARK
Robin's Wood
200 Oak Grove Road
Marshall, NC 28753

DON DANIELS
P.O. Box 939
Locust Grove, OK 74352

NONA DONOHO
75 Appian Way
Arden, NC 28704

CARLA FILIPPELLI
Cranberry Creek Baskets
423 Bob Barnwell Road
Asheville, NC 28803

DAN FREDERICKS
P.O. Box 15941
Asheville, NC 28813

RALPH GATES
8 Willow Creek Road
Leicester, NC 28748

HAROLD HALL
1203 Lake Martin Drive
Kent, OH 44240

BOBBY HANSSON
Leaping Beaver Tinker Shop
Box 1100
Rising Sun, MD 21911

PAULA HEDRICK
686 Christian Creek Road
Swannanoa, NC 28778

ROLF HOLMQUIST
900 Sparmill Road
Burnsville, NC 28714

MARIE HUDSON
102 Fairway Drive
Asheville, NC 28805

ELMA JOHNSON
12 Hollyridge Road
Asheville, NC 28803

**ELAINE KNOLL,
GLADYS SMITH,
AND BOB KNOLL**
Green Valley Woodcrafts
P.O. Box 398
Leicester, NC 28748

LADY SLIPPER DESIGNS
Route 3, Box 556
Bemidji, MN 56601

STEVE MITCHELL
76 Chinquapin Trail
Fairview, NC 28730

CHUCK O'CONNELL
Weaverville, NC

CLAUDIA AND BOB OSBY
315 W. Main
Brevard, NC 28712

MIMI SCHLEICHER
34 Wall Street
Asheville, NC 28801

**AUSTIN AND FRENCH
SCONYERS-SNOW**
Asheville, NC

RANDY SEWELL
38 Muscogee Avenue
Atlanta, GA 30305

FRANK SOUTHECORVO
20 Friendly Hollow Street
Asheville, NC 28801

MARK STROM
Lothlorian
244B Swannanoa River Road
Asheville, NC 28805

CAROL SUTHERLAND
Heathmere Pottery
Rte. 7, Honeysuckle Drive
Greenville, SC 29609

TYGRE
Asheville, NC

SUE WHEELER
405 Upper Glady Fork Road
Candler, NC 28715

CREDITS

A SPECIAL THANKS TO THE PEOPLE AROUND ASHEVILLE, NORTH CAROLINA, WHO ALLOWED US TO USE THEIR GARDENS AND YARDS AS LOCATIONS FOR TAKING PHOTOGRAPHS:

Barbara and Lew Applebaum

Curry and John Jamison

John and Dodie King

Susan and Allen Roderick

Thanks also to the folks at the Purple Martin Conservation Association, Edinboro University of Pennsylvania, Edinboro, PA 16444; Western North Carolina Nature Center for their hospitality; Hilary Vinson at the Asheville Endangered Species Field Office, U.S. Fish and Wildlife Service, for help with photographs; Richard Freudenberger, executive editor of Back Home magazine for expert woodworking directions writing; Don Osby, owner of Page 1 Publications, for his drawing artistry; Kay Butt for patience and help with the ducks; and Richard Babb and Bill Duyck for willingness far beyond the ordinary to get those perfect shots. Without the design genius of Dana Irwin, this book would be far less eyepleasing.

PHOTO CREDITS

Richard Babb: projects, except as noted, and 14b, 15a, 37a, 47d, 49a, 122b

Evan Bracken: gallery, except as noted, and 20, 22, 27, 48, 85, 91, 110, 119

Carlton Burke: 37b, 47c

Tony Dills: 40, 51a

Bill E. Duyck: 36, 49b, 63b, 69, 72, 92, 96, 97, 100, 103, 108a, 126, 129b, 138

Bobby Hansson: 31, 38, 71

James E. Hill III: 79, 84

Dana Irwin: 13, 14a, 15b, 16, 17, 47b, 50, 51b, 102, 124

Bill Lea: 63a, 133

Deborah Morgenthal: 108b, 125b

Randy Sewell: 11

Merlin D. Tuttle, Bat Conservation International: 21, 25, 29, 32

U.S. Fish and Wildlife Service: 65, 68

Additional U.S. Fish and Wildlife Service photos by:

D. Biggens: 111   Tim McCabe/SCS: 125a

Thomas Goettel: 59a   Jon Nickles: 134

John & Karen Hollingsworth: 46   Tom Smylie: 62

James C. Leopold: 56, 70, 75

METRIC CONVERSION CHART

INCHES	CM	INCHES	CM
1/8	.5	9	23
1/4	1	10	26
3/8	1.25	11	28
1/2	1.5	12	31
5/8	1.75	13	33.5
3/4	2	14	36
7/8	2.25	15	38.5
1	2.5	16	41
1-1/4	3.5	17	44
1-1/2	4	18	46
1-3/4	4.5	19	49
2	5	20	51
2-1/2	6.5	21	54
3	8	22	56.5
3-1/2	9	23	59
4	10	24	62
4-1/2	11.5	25	64
5	13	26	67
5-1/2	14	27	69
6	15	28	72
7	18	29	74.5
8	21	30	77

INDEX